THE STORY OF THE BIBLE

VOLUME II: THE NEW TESTAMENT

THE STORY OF
THE BIBLE

VOLUME I: ***The Old Testament***

Text Book
Test Book
Teacher's Manual
Activity Book
Audio Dramatization
Video Lecture Series

VOLUME II: ***The New Testament***

Text Book
Test Book
Teacher's Manual
Activity Book
Audio Dramatization
Video Lecture Series

THE STORY OF
THE BIBLE

VOLUME II:
THE NEW TESTAMENT

TAN

Nihil obstat for *Bible History*: Arthur J. Scanlan, S.T.D.

Imprimatur for *Bible History*: + Patrick Cardinal Hayes
Archbishop of New York
New York City, New York
July 1, 1931

Cover and illustrations by Chris Pelicano

Maps by Abby Glazier

ISBN: 978-1-61890-650-2

Cataloging-in-Publication data on file with the Library of Congress

Printed and bound in the United States of America
TAN Books
www.TANBooks.com
Charlotte, North Carolina
2015

CONTENTS

And the Word became flesh and dwelt among us,
full of grace and truth; we have beheld his glory,
glory as of the only Son from the Father.

—*John 1:14*

THE NEW TESTAMENT

The Story of the Bible will take you through the adventures of both Testaments, in two volumes. This first volume covers the Old Testament, and the second volume covers the New Testament.

INTRODUCTION

Your Time Has Come

Get ready for an adventure.

Open your mind and stretch your imagination. Soon we'll travel back in time to trace the origins of the universe and of the human race. Through the power of a Book unlike any other book, we can journey to a distant age, all the way back to the first age.

By the time this voyage is complete, you'll arrive back home in the present day. But what you learn along the way will help you understand better your unique place in today's world. And it will allow you to look forward, with hope and wonder, to the world to come.

Your ancestors before you, those who lived in the days of old, once sat by firelight as they studied and learned from this Book. It's filled with tales of adventure, betrayal, vengeance, war, love, heroism, and hope. As you embark on this journey, you'll come to know men and women of great holiness, and some of great wickedness as well. You'll encounter angels and demons, kings and queens, warriors and prophets—and everyday people like yourself, all with a story to tell.

Your time has come to learn this story. *It's your turn now.* You must take this Book, the one we call the Bible, and learn everything there is to know about it. Think of it as a flaming torch that has been carried through the long, dark nights of human history, a torch that has now been passed to you. Take it, steady it, and move forward with its knowledge and wisdom, so that one day you can pass it on to the ones who follow you.

But before you take up this torch, burning with the power of God's Word, it's important to understand why our heavenly Father gave it to us.

The Book of Nature

God created us to know Him, love Him, and serve Him in this world, so that we can be happy with Him forever in the world to come. The better we know Him, the more we'll love Him; and the more we love Him, the more eager we'll be to do His holy will.

For this reason, the most important lessons we must learn are those that help us to know more and more about God.

We can learn many things about God from the world around us. The radiant stars, moon, and sun that light the sky; the fragrant forests and pastures, dotted with blossoms; the towering mountains and vast deserts—all these were made by God. They are *beautiful*, so they tell us that the God who made them is *beautiful*.

The mighty rivers flow, and the great waterfalls come crashing down. The ocean tides rise and fall, and no one can resist them. Storms come thundering with lightning and gale winds. All these are *powerful*, so they tell us that the God who made them is *powerful*.

Our families and friends are kind and good to us. They watch over us lovingly and take care of our needs. So they show us that the God who made them is *loving and caring.*

In all these ways, the world tells us about our God. Since He's the One who created it, we might think of Him as an Author, and the world as His Book. Just as an author writes words on a page, so God writes with his divine Hand on the sky, the land, the sea, and the people of our world. Each morning when we open our eyes, we're able to read from this "Book of Nature" that He's written.

Even so, we need more than this "book" all around us to understand who God is and how He wants us to live. That's because we aren't always able to read correctly the wonderful lessons that are found in the Book of Nature. The things of this world are so beautiful and powerful and good that we may be tempted to think more of them than we do of the God who made them. We may end up loving them more than we love God.

But there's another reason as well why we need more than the Book of Nature to learn about God. We find that many important things about God and His will for us aren't written in that book. Some truths are above and beyond nature, and we call these *supernatural.*

God knows these truths because He is all-wise and knows all things. He wants to share them with us. Why? If we learn these supernatural truths, we'll know how to love and serve Him in a nobler way. And that will make us far happier than we could ever be if we had to depend on the Book of Nature alone.

Why We Have the Bible

For this reason, God gave us another book, which we call the Bible. It helps us make sense of the lessons that are written in the Book of Nature, as well as many other things that otherwise we could never know or understand about God, ourselves, and the world around us.

Children can't understand everything that adults can, but even the wisest adult can never understand certain things in the mind of God. They are simply too far beyond us, too complex, too vast, for us to grasp. So we must trust in Him when He tells us that something is true.

How can we trust that everything God says is true? Because He knows all things, and He cannot lie. The truths that we can't fully understand, even after God has told them to us, we call *mysteries*.

The Bible was written by men who were chosen by God especially for that purpose. These men wrote down what God wanted them to write, and nothing else. He guided them so they would not make a mistake. He brought to their memories the truths they had learned, and He placed thoughts in their minds that would never have come to them otherwise. The help that God gave to these sacred writers we call *divine inspiration*.

After Christ ascended into heaven, God inspired some of His apostles and disciples to write down many of the things He had said and done. God watched over them and guided them, making sure they would write all that He wanted them to write. After the generation of the apostles, no one ever had that special gift of divine inspiration again. By that time, God had revealed to us all the truths that are necessary for us to enter into the kingdom of heaven and to live with Him forever.

The Church that Christ founded guards the truths that He revealed. It's like a castle built to protect a great spring of life-giving water. When the spring is protected, the living water can flow out from it to all those who come to drink.

Christ promised to be with His Church—the King in His castle—until the end of time. Through this promise, we know that the Church cannot make a mistake when she tells us what we must believe and do if we wish to know, love, and serve God, both in this life and the next. Because the Church cannot make a mistake in these matters, we say she is *infallible.*

The Parts of the Bible

The Bible is divided into two parts: the *Old Testament* and the *New Testament.* The word "testament" means an agreement, or more exactly, a *covenant.* When two persons enter into a covenant, they promise to give themselves to each other in love and to be faithful in that love. Marriage is one clear example of what we mean by a covenant.

The forty-six books of the Old Testament tell us about the covenant between God and His people before Jesus came into the world. The Old Testament shows us again and again how God loved His covenant people faithfully, even when they broke the covenant and failed to love Him in return. These books tell how God promised us a Redeemer who would save us from our sins, and how He chose a certain nation, the Jews, to prepare the world for the Redeemer's coming.

The New Testament contains twenty-seven books. It tells how God's promise was fulfilled in Our Lord and Savior, Jesus Christ, and in the Church that He founded.

The Bible, then, is one large book, made up of seventy-three smaller ones.

The books in the Bible are not all alike. Some tell the story of things that happened in the past, called historical books. Others contain rules of conduct for how to live properly, called moral books. Others foretell things that will happen in the future, called prophetic books. Some of the books are even written in poetry rather than prose.

The Story of the Bible will take you through the adventures of both Testaments, in two volumes. The first volume covers the Old Testament, and this second volume covers the New Testament.

Scripture and Tradition

We should note one last thing about the truths God has revealed. Even though *Sacred Scripture*—another name for the Bible—is essential for knowing about God, other truths that He wanted us to know were not written down there. Instead, they have come to us by word of mouth and by example, beginning with the preaching and practice of the apostles. Since the time of Jesus, each generation has received these truths and handed them down to the next generation. We call this the *Sacred Tradition.*

We shouldn't be surprised that the Bible can't contain the entire teaching of the Sacred Tradition. Think only, for example, of the life of Our Lord, so full of wonderful teachings and deeds. In the Gospels, we read about many events from Jesus' life. But at the end of the Gospel of John, we're told that there were many other things Jesus said and did. If they all were written down, St. John insists, the whole world couldn't hold the books that would have to be written!

PART ONE

How Christ Prepared to Redeem the World

CHAPTER 1

The World Into Which the Messiah Came

God's Surprising Plan

God could have chosen to send His Son into the world at any time, at any place, and among any people of His choosing. Our Lord could have been born in a great and famous city, to a wealthy and influential family, in a powerful nation. He could have been born today, when modern communications media could have announced His birth around the world within minutes. But that was not heaven's plan.

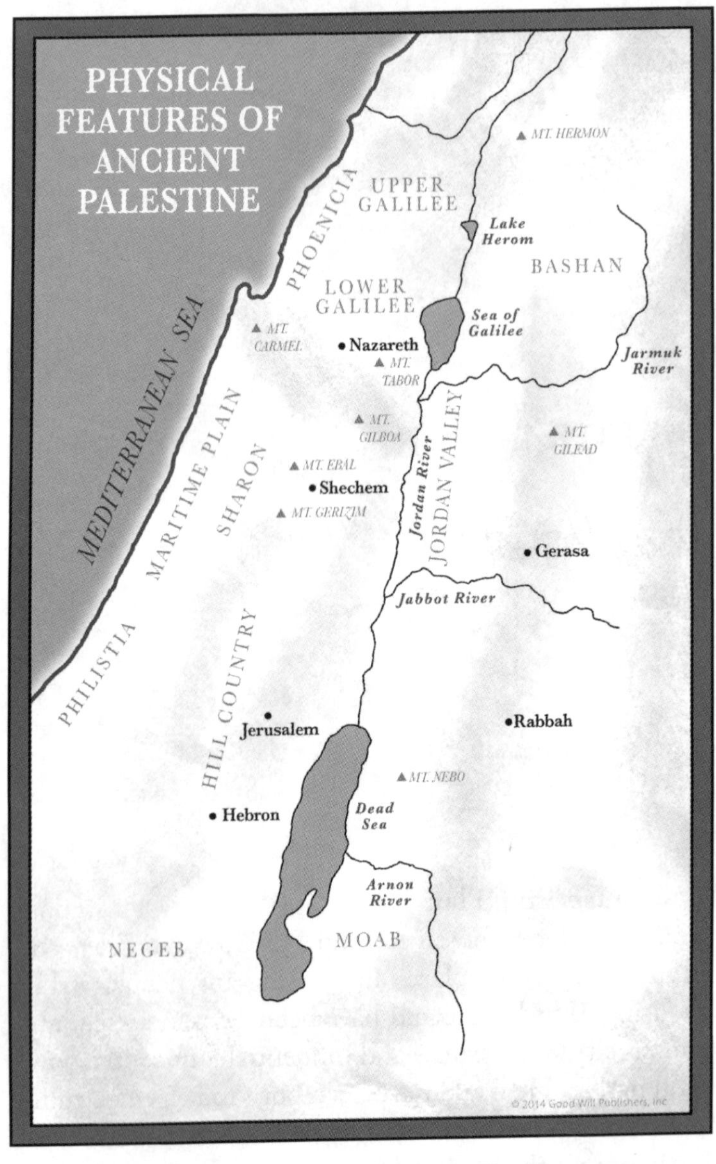
PHYSICAL FEATURES OF ANCIENT PALESTINE
MT. HERMON
UPPER GALILEE
PHOENICIA
Lake Herom
BASHAN
LOWER GALILEE
Sea of Galilee
MEDITERRANEAN SEA
MT. CARMEL
Nazareth
MT. TABOR
Jarmuk River
MT. GILBOA
MT. GILEAD
MARITIME PLAIN
SHARON
MT. EBAL
Shechem
MT. GERIZIM
Jordan River
JORDAN VALLEY
Gerasa
Jabbot River
PHILISTIA
HILL COUNTRY
Jerusalem
Rabbah
MT. NEBO
Hebron
Dead Sea
Arnon River
NEGEB
MOAB
© 2014 Good Will Publishers, Inc

Instead, the Son of God was born to a humble peasant woman unknown to anyone but her friends and neighbors. He was laid in a borrowed feeding trough, in a humble stable with dusty, smelly animals. And His infant cries first rang out in a small town in the land of a powerless people, who were despised and oppressed by the mighty men of their day.

Jesus Christ, God's Son, was born about two thousand years ago in the land of Palestine. It was the homeland that God had promised to His chosen people, the Jews. They had lived there for centuries, and at one time they had been a great nation. But their history came to be filled with terrible tragedies as they struggled, and often failed, to be faithful to the Lord.

Over the centuries, it had become abundantly clear that the Chosen People—and the whole world as well—desperately needed the Savior that God had promised to send them. Let's take a look now at the world into which He was born.

The Land of Palestine

At the time Our Lord was born, Palestine was about the same size as the state of Maryland in the United States today. West of the Jordan River, which flows through the middle of the country from north to south, were three provinces: *Galilee, Samaria,* and *Judea.*

The principal towns of Galilee, the northernmost province, were *Capernaum, Tiberias, Chorazin, Cana,* and *Nazareth.*

In Samaria, the central province, were three major cities. *Shechem* was the first capital of the rebel kings after the kingdom of Solomon had divided. *Sebaste* was the name that Herod had given to the city of Samaria, the last capital of the Northern Kingdom, after he had rebuilt it. *Caesarea* was a port on the Mediterranean Sea built by Herod.

Jerusalem, Bethlehem, Jericho, and *Arimathea* were the principal cities of Judea, the southernmost province.

On the other side of the Jordan, to the southeast, was the country known as *Perea,* whose principal city was *Pella.* Not many Jews lived in this part of Palestine during the time of Our Lord. The northeastern part of this country was divided into several provinces.

Shortly after they had gained control of Palestine, the Romans built ten cities in this region. The neighborhood of these ten cities was known as the *Decapolis,* which means "ten cities."

Palestine and Rome

Palestine was now a part of the Roman Empire. The Romans didn't govern it directly, but through rulers whom they approved. When our Savior was born, the first of four rulers by the name of Herod was the king of Palestine. Now known as *Herod the Great,* he was an Edomite appointed by the Roman ruler Julius Caesar. The people resented him because of his great cruelty, and also because he wasn't a Jew.

After the death of this Herod, his kingdom was divided among his three sons, Archelaus, Herod Antipas, and Herod Philip. Archelaus governed Judea and Samaria; Herod Antipas was ruler of Galilee and Perea; and Herod Philip governed the territories east of the Jordan.

Ten years after the death of Herod the Great, the Romans took the government of Samaria and Judea away from Archelaus because he had shown himself incapable of ruling wisely. In his place they put a *procurator,* or governor. This procurator was a Roman and had his headquarters at Caesarea. He visited Jerusalem only on the occasion of the great Jewish festivals.

The Romans kept a garrison of soldiers on guard in

the city of Jerusalem. They were stationed in the *Antonia,* a fortified building northwest of the Temple. Whenever the procurator was in Jerusalem, he lived in a palace that had been built by Herod the Great on Mount Zion, across the valley from the Temple. Between the Antonia and the Temple was a large square or court called *Gabbatha.* In this square the procurator met the people on certain occasions.

The Jews were compelled to pay taxes to Rome. The Romans sold the privilege of collecting these taxes to tax collectors. The tax collectors tried to enrich themselves at the expense of the Jews. They oppressed the people and forced them to pay as large a tax as possible.

The people hated the tax collectors, not only because they oppressed them, but also because they were a constant reminder that the Jews were no longer an independent nation, but were under the domination of a foreign power. Most of all, they despised those tax collectors who were Jews, for they considered them traitors to their nation.

Roman money was used throughout Palestine. The Roman coin most commonly mentioned in the Bible was the *denarius.* Four Roman *denarii* made one Jewish *shekel.*

The changing value of our coins today makes it difficult to compare them to these ancient coins. But we can gain some idea of their value when we note that the *denarius* was a day's wage for a common laborer of the time.

Greek coins were also in use in Palestine. A Greek *stater* was equal to the Jewish shekel. The Greek *drachma* was equal to the denarius, and the *didrachma* was equal to two drachmas. These are the kinds of coins that were entrusted to Judas for the support of the apostles. Finally, the *talent* mentioned in the Gospel was more than fifteen years' wages for a laborer.

Only Jewish money was permitted to be offered for sacrifices in the Temple. The role of the moneychangers there was to exchange Jewish coins for the people's Greek and Roman coins.

Everyday Life in Palestine

Some aspects of life in Palestine had changed very little from the time of Joshua to the time of Our Lord. People wore a cotton or linen sleeveless garment reaching to the knees, called a *tunic.* Over this was worn a long-sleeved loose garment open at the front and bound at the waist with a belt.

The outermost garment consisted of a long, loose robe with or without wide sleeves, and striped with various colors. The most popular colors were white, purple, red, and violet. Around their heads the men wore a piece of wool wrapped in the style of a turban, and the women wore a veil. On their feet they wore sandals.

The houses of the Jews were built mostly of stones piled one upon another. Hardened clay served the purpose of mortar. The house usually had one room and was one story high. It had a flat roof with a railing around it, which served as an outside deck. The floors were either unpaved earth or roughly polished stones.

The wealthy people had chairs and couches made of fine cedar wood, beautifully carved. The common people had rough benches and tables made of pine. For beds, the Jews used a thin mattress with one or two coverings, which was laid on the floor. Other common household items were little clay lamps, which burned olive oil; various wooden kitchen utensils; bottles made of skins; clay pitchers; and a hand mill for grinding grain.

The wealthier people had plates, knives, bowls, and cups made of gold, while the poor had to settle for stone and clay vessels. The meals of the rich included exotic foods brought by merchants from all parts of the Roman Empire. The poor ate lamb, fish, bread, and such fruits and vegetables as Palestine produced.

It was the custom of the time for the people to recline on cushions on the floor around dishes of food set in the middle, much like spokes around the hub of a wheel. They ate with their fingers from a common dish.

Because the climate was hot and the roads dusty, the Jews bathed often. They also anointed their skin with oil. Before coming into the house or sitting down at table or going to bed, they washed their feet.

Among the Jews were tradesmen of every kind, carpenters, masons, jewelers, tailors, and shoemakers. There were also shopkeepers who sold food, clothing, and furniture. But most of the people in Judea made their living by herding sheep and cattle or tilling the soil. In Galilee, the people typically lived by fishing and farming. In Samaria, they lived chiefly by farming.

They had no threshing machines in those days, but after the wheat was cut down, the sheaves were brought to a threshing floor. There, oxen trampled them and loosened the grain from the stock.

Usually there was a breeze in the evening. That's when the farmer used the threshing fork, which looked like a wide wooden fork with a short handle. With this he tossed the wheat into the air. The grain, being heavier, fell to the ground, while the chaff was blown away.

A day for the Jews lasted from sunset to sunset. The "first hour," as they called it, was 6 a.m.; the third hour, 9 a.m.; the sixth hour, noon; the ninth hour, 3 p.m.; and the twelfth hour, 6 p.m.

In the time of Christ, four languages were used in Palestine. The Sacred Books were written in ancient Hebrew, which few of the Jews understood. The language used in everyday life was Aramaic.

Usually those in high positions, and many of the Galileans, knew Greek. Since the time of Alexander's conquest, Greek had become an international language for people living in the lands he had conquered. A few also knew Latin, since it was the language of the Romans. Public signs and notices were often written in Aramaic, Greek, and Latin, so that all might be able to read them.

Religious Life

Every morning and evening a lamb was sacrificed at the Temple to acknowledge God's ownership of all things. Special sacrifices were offered on the great feast days. The *Feast of the Pasch* (or *Passover*) and the *Feast of Weeks* were observed in spring. The *Day of Atonement* and the *Feast of Tabernacles* (or *Booths*) were observed in September.

Two feasts had been added to the Jewish calendar after the time of Moses. These were the *Feast of Purim,* celebrated in February to commemorate the day when Queen Esther saved her people in Persia; and the *Feast of the Dedication,* observed in November in honor of the rededication of the altar and the Temple by Judas Maccabeus. This Jewish feast is known today as *Hanukah.* On the first day of every month as well, special religious ceremonies were conducted for the people.

Though the Jews were under the power of the Roman emperor, they were allowed to govern themselves in many things. For this purpose, they had the *Sanhedrin,* which was a body of seventy-one members. To this council belonged the *chief priests,* as the former high priests were called; the *elders,* who were the leading men of the people; and the *scribes,* who were specialists in religious law. The council was presided over by the current *high priest,* who was usually appointed by the ruler of the country.

The Sanhedrin met in one of the halls of the Temple. It had authority over all religious matters in the land. It controlled the public worship, saw that the Law of Moses was carried out properly, and decided which prophets were true and which were false. It was a kind of supreme court that could pass judgment on those who were found guilty of disobeying the Law. However, it had no right to condemn anyone to death. This power was reserved to the Roman procurator.

Since the Temple in Jerusalem had been rebuilt, sacrifices were offered only there, as the Law of Moses required. But as we noted before, during the time of their exile the Jews had developed the custom of gathering together in local *synagogues,* for worship, religious instruction, and the reading of Scripture. This custom was maintained by the Jews who returned to Judea from exile, and these synagogues now served also as schools and courthouses. They were found throughout Palestine and in other parts of the world, wherever Jews gathered to worship.

Every synagogue had its ruler and elders. The rulers had the power to "cast out of the synagogue" those members they declared unworthy. The people "cast out" were no longer considered part of the religious community.

The duty of instructing the people in the Law of Moses, and of translating and explaining the Scriptures to them, had become a special profession in the time of Our Lord. The men who performed this duty were known as *scribes.* In the Bible they are also called *lawyers.*

Religious Parties

The *Pharisees* were a sect that had been formed after the Jews returned from captivity. Their purpose was to preserve the Sacred Scriptures and to keep them free from error. They were deeply patriotic and tried to keep alive the ancient traditions of the people.

In the beginning, they had done splendid work and had brought about a great reform in the conduct of the Jews. But as time went on, many Pharisees became more interested in the letter of the Law than in its spirit. They had a high opinion of themselves and made a great show of their carefulness in observing every detail of the Law of Moses.

The Pharisees often despised those who didn't observe the Law as they did. At the hours of prayer they recited long prayers in public and wore on their foreheads or arms larger *phylacteries* than the other Jews wore, to make a show of their religious practice. These phylacteries were bands of parchment containing sacred texts.

Most of the scribes were Pharisees. But some scribes belonged to other religious parties.

Opposed to the Pharisees were the *Sadducees.* They denied some of the teachings found in the Jewish Scriptures that had been written in later centuries than the others. They didn't believe, for example, in angels, the resurrection of the body, or the life of the world to come.

The Sadducees ridiculed the Pharisees for their strictness in keeping the law. Many of them belonged to the wealthy classes and imitated the fashions of Greece and Rome. Some of them belonged to the court of Herod the Great; in contempt, the people called them *Herodians.*

The high priest sometimes belonged to the party of the

Sadducees, as did most of the members of the Sanhedrin. They tended to be worldly men who followed the external observances of the Law only because they feared the people. They also tended to be more politically active and accepted the Roman domination of their land.

The *Essenes* were another sect that had grown up after the Jews returned from captivity. They lived apart from the people in communities governed by strict rules, very much like certain monks of our day.

The *Nazarites* were a class of men who took a vow to serve God by a life of penance and mortification. They had existed among the Chosen People since the days of Moses. During the time he was bound by his vow, the Nazarite was not allowed to drink intoxicating liquor or to cut his hair. He was not permitted to approach dead bodies.

How Judeans Saw Galileans and Samaritans

Though the Jewish people of Galilee usually lived according to the Law of Moses, they were not held in very high esteem by the people of Judea. Some of them were fishermen, but most of them worked small farms. They spoke a distinctive dialect and were not as highly cultured as the people of Judea. In addition, many pagans lived in Galilee, so the Judeans looked down on the region.

The people of Samaria, called *Samaritans*, had a religion of their own that differed from that of the rest of the Jews. Their Bible consisted only of the first five books of our Bible. They had their own temple on Mount Gerizim, which they insisted was the only temple of the true God.

The people of Judea and Galilee avoided them. They refused to pass through Samaritan territory unless it was absolutely necessary. They wouldn't even ask Samaritans for a drink of water if they were thirsty, because they refused to drink out of the same vessels as Samaritans.

Herod's Temple

In the time of Our Lord, the great Temple at Jerusalem was spoken of as *Herod's Temple,* because Herod the Great rebuilt it after it had been partially destroyed by fire during a siege of Jerusalem. It had the same three main divisions as the earlier temple: the *Porch, the Holy Place,* and the *Holy of Holies.*

The Porch was on the east side. It was one hundred and fifty feet high, much like a great hall with three rows of beautiful columns running its whole length. The entrance to the Porch was through beautifully decorated gates.

The Temple itself was made up of the *Holy Place* and the *Holy of Holies.* Surrounding the Temple and on a lower level was the large *Court of the Priests,* which only priests and Levites were permitted to enter. In it was the altar of sacrifice. On the north, south, and west of this was the *Court of the Israelites,* which all Jewish men might enter. East of this was the *Court of the Women,* which Jewish women were allowed to enter.

Surrounding the Court of the Israelites and the Court of the Women was the *Court of the Gentiles.* It was separated from the other courts by a wall four and a half feet high. There were openings in this wall to allow the Jews to enter or leave the other courts.

Near these openings were signs in Latin and in Greek warning all those who were not Jews that they would be punished by death if they entered within the enclosure. This Court of the Gentiles became in many ways a market place, where animals for the sacrifices were bought and sold, and where the moneychangers had their booths. It was from this Court that Christ drove out the buyers and the sellers. On the outside of this Court was a large open space, flanked on all sides by a high wall containing porches and halls. At its southeast corner was a high tower known as the *Pinnacle* of the Temple.

Knowing these aspects of life in Palestine helps us understand better the world into which our Savior was born. It also makes us familiar with a number of terms used in the Gospels that have to do with the objects, customs, and attitudes of everyday life and religious life. With these in mind, we can now turn to the stories of Jesus' birth, childhood, and youth.

CHAPTER 2

The Redeemer Comes to Earth

The Announcement of the Birth of John the Baptist

Not far from Jerusalem, in the hill country of Judea, lived a priest whose name was Zechariah, and his wife, Elizabeth. They belonged to the tribe of Levi, and they were righteous in the sight of God, living in obedience to the laws of the Lord. When it was his turn, Zechariah left his home and went up to Jerusalem to take part in the services of the Temple.

There was one great disappointment in the lives of Zechariah and Elizabeth. For many years they had been praying that God would allow them to have a son. But they had given up hope that God would hear them.

One day toward the end of the reign of Herod the Great, it was Zechariah's turn to serve in the Temple. He went to place incense on the Altar of Incense that stood in the Holy Place, just outside the veil of the Holy of Holies. As he was standing before the Altar, suddenly an angel appeared to him.

Zechariah was frightened, but the angel said, "Don't be afraid, Zechariah, for your prayer has been heard, and your wife, Elizabeth, will bear you a son, and you will call his name John. . . . He will be great before the Lord, and he will be filled with the Holy Spirit even in his mother's womb. And he will bring back to the Lord their God many of the children of Israel."

But Zechariah doubted the word of the angel. He said, "How will I know this to be true? For I'm an old man, and my wife is advanced in years."

The angel answered: "I am Gabriel. I stand in the presence of God, and I've been sent to speak to you and to bring you this good news. So you will be silent and unable to speak until the day that all this comes to pass, because you haven't believed my words."

Outside, the people were waiting for Zechariah, and they wondered why he stayed so long in the Temple. When he came out, he couldn't speak to them. He had to make signs to communicate. Then they understood that he had seen a vision in the Temple.

The Announcement of the Birth of Jesus

Six months later, the angel Gabriel was sent from God into a city of Galilee called Nazareth. His mission was to speak to a virgin engaged to a man whose name was Joseph, a descendant of David. The virgin's name was Mary, and she was a relative of Elizabeth.

The angel said to Mary, "Hail, full of grace! The Lord is with you; blessed are you among women." When Mary heard these words, she was troubled, and wondered what kind of greeting this could be.

But the angel said to her, "Don't be afraid, Mary, for you

have found grace with God. . . . You will conceive in your womb and bear a Son; and you will call His name Jesus.

"He will be great, and will be called the Son of the Most High. And the Lord God will give Him the throne of David His forefather; and He will reign as king over the house of Jacob forever. And of His kingdom there will be no end."

Mary said to the angel, "How will this happen, since I don't have relations with a man?"

The angel said to her, "The Holy Spirit will come upon you, and the power of the Most High will overshadow you. So the Holy One to be born will be called the Son of God. See! Your relative Elizabeth has also conceived a son in her old age . . . because nothing is impossible with God."

Then Mary said, "I am the handmaiden of the Lord; let it be done to me according to your word." And the angel departed from her.

Mary Visits Elizabeth

The knowledge that she was to be the Mother of God filled Mary's heart with happiness, but she didn't forget the great joy that had come to Elizabeth. She set out right away on the journey from Nazareth to the Judean hill country to visit her relative. It was a journey of four or five days, and she probably made it on foot.

Entering the house of Zechariah, Mary greeted Elizabeth affectionately. In that moment the Holy Spirit revealed to Elizabeth that Mary was the Mother of God, and she cried out with a loud voice: "Blessed are you among women, and blessed is the fruit of your womb. And how have I deserved to have the mother of my Lord come to me? . . . Blessed is she who believed, because the things promised her by the Lord will be accomplished."

When Mary heard these words, the joy in her heart knew no bounds. There burst from her lips the song we call the *Magnificat,* a prayer of praise and thanksgiving to the Lord. She said:

"My soul magnifies the Lord, and my spirit rejoices in God my Savior; because He has regarded the lowly estate of His handmaiden. . . . From now on, all generations will call me blessed, because He who is mighty has done great things for me, and holy is His name. And His mercy is from generation to generation on those who fear Him.

"He has shown might with His arm; He has scattered the proud in the conceit of their hearts. He has put down the mighty from their thrones, and has exalted the lowly. He has filled the hungry with good things, and the rich He has sent away empty.

"He has given help to Israel His servant, mindful of His mercy—just as He spoke to our fathers, to Abraham and to his posterity forever."

Mary stayed with Elizabeth about three months, and then she returned to her home in Nazareth.

The Birth of John the Baptist

When Elizabeth's son was born, her neighbors and relatives gathered in her house to congratulate her and to praise God, who had shown His great mercy toward her. On the eighth day the child was circumcised according to the custom of the Jews. This was a sign that he belonged to the religion of his fathers and was entitled to all its privileges.

At this ceremony the Jewish child usually received his name. The relatives wanted him to be called Zechariah after his father. But Elizabeth said, "No; he'll be called John."

"But none of your relatives are called by that name," they protested. Then they made signs to Zechariah, asking him what the child should be named. So Zechariah asked for a writing tablet.

He wrote on it, "John is his name." No sooner had he written these words than he was able to speak again, and he praised God. Everyone present was frightened by what happened, and the news spread all over the hill country of Judea. All who heard about it said, "What sort of man will this child be?" For it was clear that the Lord was with him.

Filled with the Holy Spirit, Zechariah prophesied:

"Blessed be the Lord, the God of Israel, because He has visited and redeemed His people. And He has raised up a horn of salvation for us, in the house of David His servant. As He promised through the mouth of His holy ones, the prophets from of old; salvation from our enemies, and from the hand of all who hate us, to show mercy to our forefathers, and to be mindful of His holy covenant, of the oath that He swore to Abraham our father—that He would grant us, that, delivered from the hand of our enemies, we might serve Him without fear, in holiness and justice before Him all our days.

"And you, child, will be called the prophet of the Most High; for you will go before the face of the Lord to prepare His ways, to give to His people knowledge of salvation through the forgiveness of their sins, because of the loving kindness of our God, when the Dawn from on high visits us; to shine on those who sit in darkness and in the shadow of death, to guide our feet into the way of peace."

This beautiful song is called the *Benedictus.* Today it has a prominent place in the liturgy of the Church.

Now the child of Zechariah and Elizabeth grew up strong in body and holy in spirit. To prepare for his ministry, the Lord led him to live out in the wilderness. One day God would call him to come out from there and preach to the people.

The Birth of Jesus

After Mary had returned to her home in Nazareth, Joseph learned that she was to become the mother of the Savior. An angel appeared to him in his sleep and said:

"Don't be afraid, Joseph, son of David, to take Mary

as your wife, for the Child conceived in her is of the Holy Spirit. She will bear a Son, and you will call His name Jesus; for He will save His people from their sins."

In this way the prophecy of Isaiah was fulfilled: "Behold, the virgin will be with child, and will bear a son, and they will call His name *Emmanuel,* which means, 'God with us.'"

Now in those days Augustus, the Roman emperor, issued a decree ordering that a census must be taken of his whole empire. Rome had reached the height of her power, and the emperor wanted to know more exactly the extent of his rule. The census would also reveal to him the resources of the various provinces, so he could decide how much to tax them.

Whenever the Jews took a census, they left their place of residence and went to the city from which their ancestors had come. So Joseph and Mary left the city of Nazareth in Galilee, and went to Bethlehem in Judea, the City of David. Bethlehem was King David's birthplace; and Rachel, the wife of Jacob, Abraham's grandson, was buried there.

When they reached the little town of Bethlehem, they found it crowded with visitors. There was no room for them in the inn. They sought in vain for a place to stay, but the best shelter they could find was a stable for animals.

So Joseph and Mary made preparations to remain there for the night. And it was during that night, and in that humble stable, that the Son of God was born into the world. Mary wrapped the divine Infant in swaddling clothes and laid Him in a manger, where the animals were fed.

Not far away a group of shepherds were keeping watch over their flocks at night to protect them from wolves and robbers. Suddenly an angel of the Lord appeared to them, and the brightness of heaven shone around them. The shepherds were terrified!

But the angel said to them, "Don't be afraid. Look! I bring you good news of great joy that will be to all the people. For today in the town of David a Savior has been born to you, who is Christ the Lord. And this will be a sign to you: You'll find an Infant wrapped in swaddling clothes and lying in a manger."

He had no sooner spoken than the shepherds saw with him a great multitude of angels, and heard them praising God: "Glory to God in the highest, and on earth peace among men of good will!" Then the angels disappeared.

The hearts of the shepherds were filled with wonder, and they said one to another, "Let's go over to Bethlehem and see this thing that has come to pass, which the Lord has made known to us."

They hurried to Bethlehem, and there they found Mary and Joseph, and the Baby lying in a manger. Kneeling down, they adored their Savior. Then the shepherds returned to their flocks, glorifying and praising God for all the things they had heard and seen.

Jesus Is Circumcised and Presented in the Temple

As the Law of Moses required, eight days later the Child was circumcised. He was called *Jesus,* the name spoken by the angel Gabriel when he appeared to Mary. The name means "Savior."

When the infant Jesus was forty days old, Mary and Joseph carried Him to Jerusalem where, according to the Law of Moses, He was to be presented to the Lord. While they were offering the sacrifice that the Law required of the poor—a pair of turtledoves or two young pigeons—the Holy Spirit led a man named Simeon into the Temple.

Simeon lived in Jerusalem. He was an old man, holy and devout, who throughout his long life had prayed and waited for the Savior. The Holy Spirit had answered his prayer and promised him that he would not die before he had seen Christ the Lord.

When he saw the infant Jesus, he took Him in his arms, blessed God and said, "Lord, now let Your servant depart in peace, according to Your word, because my eyes have seen Your salvation, which You have prepared in the presence of all peoples; a light of revelation to the Gentiles, and the glory of Your people Israel." This canticle, called *Nunc Dimittis,* appears in the Church's liturgy today.

Then turning to Mary and Joseph, Simeon blessed them. To Mary he said, "This Child is destined for the fall and for the rise of many in Israel, and for a sign that will be contradicted. And a sword will pierce your own soul, so that the thoughts of many hearts may be revealed."

There was also in the Temple a prophetess, named Anna. She was an elderly widow, but she stayed in the Temple night and day, praying and fasting. When she saw the infant Jesus, she knew at once that He was the Savior of the world, and she announced His coming to all who were hoping for the redemption of Israel.

The Wise Men

While the Child was still quite young, wise men, called *magi,* came from the East to Jerusalem, seeking the King of the Jews. They studied the stars, and they had seen His star in the East, announcing a royal birth. So they had come to adore Him.

When King Herod heard this, he was troubled, because he wanted no rivals for his throne. So he assembled all the chief priests and the scribes of the people and asked them about the ancient prophecies that told of a coming royal *Messiah,* or the *Christ,* which means "the One anointed" by God.

Herod demanded to know where this Christ would be born. They replied, "In Bethlehem in Judea, for so it is written by the prophet: 'And you, Bethlehem, in the land of Judah, are by no means least among the princes of Judah, for from you will come a Leader who will rule My people Israel.'"

When he learned from them that this King of the Jews was to be born at Bethlehem, he called the wise men privately to ask when the star of the new King had appeared. Then Herod sent them off to Bethlehem and told them to return to Jerusalem when they found the Child. He said that he, too, wanted to adore Him.

Of course, Herod was lying. His true intention was to find the Baby and kill Him.

When the wise men learned from Herod where to look for the Child, they set out for Bethlehem. As they left Jerusalem, the star that had guided them in the East went before them again, until it stood over the place where the Child laid.

The wise men entered the house and found the Child and His Mother. Falling down, they adored Him. They opened their treasures and offered Him gifts of gold, frankincense, and myrrh.

Later, they were warned in a dream not to go back to Herod. So they returned home by another way.

The Flight to Egypt

When the wise men had gone, an angel of the Lord appeared to Joseph in his sleep. He told him to get up, take the Child and His mother, and flee to Egypt. They were to remain there until he received word to return, because Herod would be searching for the Child to destroy Him.

So Joseph got up and obeyed the Lord's instructions immediately. He started out on the journey to Egypt with Jesus and Mary in the middle of the night.

Herod waited in vain for the wise men to return to him. When at last he realized that they weren't coming, he was furious. He sent soldiers into Bethlehem and to all the country around it, with orders to kill every little boy who was two years old or younger. In this way he hoped to destroy the newborn King of the Jews.

The soldiers entered Bethlehem, tore the babies from their mothers' arms, and murdered them. This horror fulfilled the prophecy of Jeremiah, who had said long before, "A voice . . . was heard, weeping and loud lamentation; Rachel weeping for her children, and she would not be comforted, because they are no more."

The Holy Family lived in Egypt until Herod died. Then the angel appeared to Joseph and said, "Get up, and take the Child and His mother, and go to the land of Israel. For those who sought the Child's life are dead." So Joseph returned to Israel. In this way the words of the prophet were fulfilled: "Out of Egypt have I called My Son."

Hearing that Archelaus, Herod's son, was reigning in Judea in the place of his father, Joseph was afraid to return to Bethlehem. Archelaus was following in his father's footsteps, treating the Jews with great cruelty. In obedience to a warning that came to him in a dream, Joseph took Jesus and Mary back to their home at Nazareth, in Galilee. Again, the word of the prophet was fulfilled that had said, "He will be called a Nazarene."

Nazareth was a town of about fifteen thousand people, in the southern part of Galilee. From the surrounding hills could be seen the Plain of Esdraelon, and in the distance the Mediterranean Sea and Mount Carmel. To the north were the snowcapped peaks of Lebanon and Hermon; to the east were Mount Tabor, the low riverbed of the Jordan, and the tableland of Gilead.

The country around Nazareth was fertile. Flowers grew everywhere, and the mild climate helped in the raising of pomegranates, oranges, figs, and olives.

Here it was that Jesus lived for thirty years. He was kind and obedient to Mary and Joseph, and the Bible says He advanced in wisdom and age and grace with God and men. But we're told no further details about his earliest years.

Finding Jesus in the Temple

Every year in the springtime, Mary and Joseph went up to Jerusalem to celebrate the great Feast of the Passover. When Jesus was twelve years old, He went along with them. The celebration of this feast lasted seven days. When it was over, Mary and Joseph began their journey home, but the Child Jesus remained in Jerusalem, though His parents didn't know it. They must have thought He was with some friend or with one of their relatives.

Great crowds of pilgrims were in the city of Jerusalem for the celebration of the Passover, so it's easy to understand why there would be so much confusion when they set out on their journey home. Usually the men traveled in one company, and the women in another. Extended families, with aunts and uncles and cousins, took part. So children might be with their fathers or with their mothers, or with their cousins' families. Only after they had gone quite a distance from the city would the families be united.

At the end of the first day's journey, Mary and Joseph looked for Jesus among their relatives and acquaintances. But He was not to be found. Fearing that something had happened to Him, and filled with sorrow, they hurried back to Jerusalem.

They searched throughout the city looking for Him, but all in vain. They were frantic. Then at last, on the third day after His disappearance, they found Him in the Temple, sitting among the doctors of the Law of Moses, listening to them and asking them questions. All who heard Him were amazed at His wisdom and His answers.

Mary and Joseph were surprised when they saw Jesus conversing with all these highly educated men. Going up to Him, Mary said, "Son, why have you done this to us? Look! Your father and I have searched for you, grieving."

But Jesus said to her, "Why did you search for Me? Didn't you know that I must be in My Father's house?" Then Jesus, Mary, and Joseph left Jerusalem and started on their journey to Nazareth.

No other incidents in Jesus' life are reported in Scripture from the years between His finding in the Temple and the beginning of His public ministry. We can conclude, however, that at some time during these years, Joseph died. The Bible doesn't report his death. But he's never mentioned again in the Gospels, and surely he would have been with Mary, close to Jesus in His work as an adult, if he were still alive at that time.

In any case, we can imagine how tenderly Jesus and Mary watched over him and took care of him in his last days, and how happy he was to die in their arms. After his passing, we can be sure that the home of the Holy Family remained a loving, peaceful place. But the day would come when Mary would watch, with a mixture of joy and sadness, as Jesus left home to launch out into His ministry for the salvation of the world.

PART TWO

How Christ Ministered

CHAPTER 3

Christ Begins His Public Ministry

John the Baptist Prepares the Way

Out in the desert, John, the son of Zechariah, was getting ready for the great work to which God had called him. He lived the life of a Nazarite, wearing a rough garment made of camel's hair, with a leather belt around his waist. The only food he ate was locusts and the wild honey that the bees deposited in the crevices of rocks or in hollow trees. When God revealed to him that the time had come for him to begin his work, he came out of the desert into the country along the Jordan River and began to preach to the people.

There was a ford in the Jordan, and all day long people were crossing it on their travels to or from Jerusalem. John stood near this ford, and as the people were passing by, he called out to them, saying, "Repent, for the kingdom of heaven is at hand!"

Hearing these strange words, the people would stop and ask him what he meant. He would begin preaching to them and telling them to be sorry for their sins. The very sight of him was enough to move their hearts to repentance.

They remembered the words of the prophet Isaiah: "A voice of one crying in the desert: Prepare the way of the Lord; make straight His paths. Every valley will be filled, and every mountain and hill will be brought low; and the crooked ways will be made straight, and the rough ways plain; and all mankind will see the salvation of God."

In the beginning, John's audiences were small. But soon the story of this strange preacher traveled throughout the land, and great crowds came to the Jordan to hear him. Many were converted by his words. They went out and stood in the river, where he baptized them as a sign of their repentance and their resolution to live a better life. This baptism did not wash away their sins, but it prepared their hearts for the coming of the Savior.

The people regarded John, whom they called the Baptist, as a great prophet. Not since the days of the prophets of old had anyone spoken with such authority.

Many of the Pharisees and Sadducees went to hear him. To them, John said, "You brood of vipers! Who has shown you how to flee from the wrath to come? Bring forth fruits worthy of repentance. . . . Every tree that doesn't bring forth good fruit is to be cut down and thrown into the fire."

Some tax collectors came to him to be baptized, asking, "Master, what are we to do?"

He answered, “Collect no more than what has been appointed you”; that is, take only the amount of tax that is just.

To the soldiers who came and asked what they should do, he said, “Don’t plunder, don’t accuse anyone falsely, and be content with your pay.”

To the ordinary people who feared God and tried to do their duty, he said, “Whoever has two coats, let him give to the one who has none. And whoever has food, let him do the same.”

Many of the people began to wonder in their hearts whether John might perhaps be the Savior. But John said to them, "I baptize you with water. But there will come One mightier than I am, and I am unworthy even to loosen the strap of His sandals. He will baptize you with the Holy Spirit and with fire.

"His threshing fork is in His hand, and He will clean out His threshing floor and will gather the wheat into His barn. But the chaff He will burn with unquenchable fire."

The Baptism of Jesus

When Jesus was thirty years old, He left Nazareth and came to the Jordan where John was preaching. He asked to be baptized. Knowing that Jesus was the Messiah and was without sin, John said to Him, "I ought to be baptized by You, yet You come to me?"

Jesus explained to John that He must be baptized because it was part of God's plan for redeeming the human race. Humbly John obeyed, and he baptized the Savior of the world.

When Jesus came out of the water, the heavens were opened and the Holy Spirit came down on Him in the form of a dove. A voice from heaven was heard, saying, "This is My beloved Son, in whom I am well pleased. Listen to Him!"

After His baptism, Jesus was led by the Spirit of God into the northern part of the desert of Judea, one of the roughest of all the deserts in Palestine. Here the Savior hid Himself away for forty days, praying and fasting in preparation for the great work that lay ahead. He had no companions except the wild animals of the desert. For forty days and forty nights, He ate and drank nothing.

After the long fast, Jesus was hungry. Satan appeared to Him in the desert and said, "If you are the Son of God, command this stone to become a loaf of bread."

But Jesus answered, "Man does not live by bread alone, but by every word that proceeds from the mouth of God."

Then the Devil took Him up into Jerusalem and set Him on the pinnacle of the Temple. He said, "If you are the Son of God, throw Yourself down from here, for it is written, 'He will give His angels charge over you, to guard you,' and 'In their hands they will bear you up, so that you may not strike your foot against a stone.'"

But Jesus answered, "You shall not tempt the Lord your God."

Finally, the Devil took Jesus up onto a high mountain and showed Him all the kingdoms of the world and their glory. He said to Him, "All these will I give you, if you fall down and worship me."

Then Jesus said to him, "Go away, Satan, for it is written: 'You shall worship the Lord your God, and Him only shall you serve.'" Then the Devil left Him, and angels came and took care of Him.

Jesus Calls His First Disciples

When Jesus left the desert after His fast of forty days, he went back to the Jordan, where John was still baptizing. When John saw Jesus coming toward him, he cried out, "Behold the Lamb of God! Behold the One who takes away the sin of the world!"

The next day John was standing on the banks of the river with two of his *disciples,* that is, his followers, and Jesus passed by again. Pointing to Him, John said again, "Behold the Lamb of God." The two disciples left John and started to follow Jesus.

Jesus turned and said to them, "What is it that you seek?"

They answered, "*Rabbi,*" which means "Teacher," "where do You live?"

Jesus replied, "Come and see." So they went along and stayed with Him all that day. Their names were John and Andrew.

Now Andrew had a brother named Simon. He went to look for him, and when he found him, he said, "We have found the Messiah." Then he took him to Jesus.

When Jesus saw Simon, He said, "You are Simon; you will be called *Cephas*." *Cephas* is the Aramaic word for "Peter," which means "a rock."

On the following day, Jesus went into Galilee and met there a young man named Philip. He said to him, "Follow Me." Shortly after this, Philip met his friend, Nathanael, and told him that he had found the Messiah, who was Jesus of Nazareth.

The city of Nazareth was looked down upon as a place of little status by some of the Jewish people. So Nathanael asked, "Can anything good come from Nazareth?"

Philip answered, "Come and see."

When Jesus saw Nathanael coming to Him, He said, "Look! A true Israelite in whom there is no deceit!"

Nathanael said to Him, "How do you know me?"

Jesus answered, "Before Philip called you, when you were under the fig tree, I saw you."

Nathanael replied, "Rabbi, You are the Son of God; You are the King of Israel."

From that time, Jesus began to preach to the people, saying, "Repent, for the kingdom of heaven is at hand." Soon great crowds were following Him wherever He went. Many of the people believed in Him and tried to live according to His teachings.

One day, when Jesus was walking by the Sea of Galilee, He saw the two brothers, Simon and Andrew. They were casting a net into the sea, for they were fishermen. He said to them, "Come, follow Me, and I'll have you fishing for men." Immediately they left their nets and followed Him.

Going a little farther on, He saw John in a boat with his brother, James, and his father, who was called Zebedee. They were mending their nets. He called them, and immediately James and John left their nets and their father, and followed Him.

Another day, as Jesus was passing by the tax office, He saw a tax collector named Matthew, collecting the taxes. Jesus said to him, "Follow Me." Right away, Matthew got up and followed Him.

Jesus Chooses His Apostles

One day, when they were in Galilee, Jesus went alone up a mountain to pray. He spent the whole night in prayer, and at dawn He came down to where His disciples were waiting for Him. Then He chose twelve of them to be His *apostles,* those who would have a special mission in establishing His Church. These twelve were to remain with Him always.

Here are their names: Simon, the fisherman to whom He gave the name Peter; James and John, the sons of Zebedee, whom he nicknamed the "Sons of Thunder"; Andrew, Peter's brother; Philip; Bartholomew, known also as Nathanael; Matthew, the tax collector; Thomas, whose name means "the twin"; James, the son of Alpheus; Thaddeus, also called Jude; Simon, called the Zealot; and Judas Iscariot. All except Judas, who came from Kerioth, a town in Judea, were Galileans. From this time forward the twelve apostles gave all their time to the service of the Savior and followed Him wherever He went.

For nine months, Jesus instructed the apostles and prepared them for their mission. Then He sent them out to work miracles and preach the *Gospel,* the good news about the salvation that Jesus had come to bring the world. Throughout Palestine they preached and worked miracles, because He gave them power to heal the sick, to raise the dead to life, and to cast out demons.

The apostles didn't preach at this time to the Gentiles or to the Samaritans, but only to the Jews. They went from city to city, without money, food, or extra clothing. Jesus instructed them to place their trust in God and depend for their living on the faith and generosity of the people to whom they preached the Gospel.

Jesus Sends Out Seventy-Two Disciples

Besides the twelve apostles, our Savior had numerous disciples. He chose seventy-two of them to be instructed and sent out to preach. Two by two, they went out into every city and place where Our Lord Himself would be coming.

Jesus said to them, "The harvest indeed is great, but the laborers are few. So pray that the Lord of the harvest will send out laborers into His harvest.

"Go your way. Look! I'm sending you out as lambs among wolves. Carry no purse, no money, no shoes. . . . Heal the sick . . . and say to them, 'The kingdom of God has come near to you.'

"Whoever hears you, hears Me, and whoever rejects you, rejects Me. And whoever rejects Me, rejects the One who sent Me."

The first missionary tour of the seventy-two disciples lasted one month. They returned to Jesus filled with delight at the success of their work, telling Him all that had happened. They boasted that even the demons were obedient to them because they came in the name of Jesus.

But Our Lord said to them, "Don't rejoice that the demons are obedient to you. Instead, rejoice in this: that your names are written in heaven."

The Death of John the Baptist

Herod Antipas, the ruler of Galilee and Perea, had unlawfully married Herodias, the wife of Philip, his half-brother. John the Baptist rebuked him for this sin publicly, so Herod ordered him thrown into prison.

At this time, Jesus had begun His public life, preaching to the people and working a number of miracles. From his prison, John sent two of his disciples to Jesus to ask Him whether or not He were the Messiah. He did this, not because he himself doubted, but to prove to his disciples that Christ was the Savior for whom they had been waiting.

Jesus replied to their question: "Go and report to John what you have heard and seen: the blind see, the lame walk, the lepers are cleansed, the deaf hear, the dead rise again, and the poor have the gospel preached to them." The prophets had declared that all these would be signs of the Messiah.

When John's disciples had gone their way, Jesus spoke about John to the crowds: "What did you go out to the desert to see? . . . A man dressed in fine clothing? Look: Those who wear fine clothes are in the houses of kings.

"So what *did* you go out to see—a prophet? Yes, I tell you, and more than a prophet. This is the One of whom it is written, 'Behold, I send My messenger before your face, who will make ready your way before you.' Among those born of women, no prophet has come who is greater than John the Baptist."

John the Baptist had been in prison about a year when Herod Antipas held a great celebration on the occasion of his birthday. All the public officials and military officers of Galilee were invited. While the guests were seated around the banquet table, Salome, the daughter of Herodias, danced as they watched. Herod was quite pleased with her, so he made an oath to give her whatever she would ask of him, even if it were half of his kingdom.

Salome asked permission to consult with her mother. Now Herodias hated John the Baptist, because he had publicly condemned her sinful behavior. So she told her daughter to ask for the head of John the Baptist on a dish.

Salome returned to the king and said to him, "Give me, on a dish, the head of John the Baptist." When Herod heard this, he was very sad. He knew that John was a holy man, for he had visited him in prison. But because of the oath he had made before all his guests, he ordered that John must be beheaded.

The head was brought to him on a dish and he gave it to Salome, who took it to her mother. In this way Herodias had her revenge. The disciples of John took the body of their master and buried it.

In the spring of the following year, Herod moved his residence to Sepphoris, a town just west of Nazareth. All the people in that part of the country were talking about the teachings and the miracles of Our Lord. Herod thought that Jesus might be John returned to life. He was afraid of Him, yet he was anxious to see the great Prophet.

But his desire was not to be satisfied until the day Our Lord was placed on trial for His life. In the meantime, Jesus had a mission to fulfill.

CHAPTER 4

Christ Calls All People to Repentance

Jesus' Goodness Attracts Followers

Wherever Jesus went, great crowds came out to see Him and to listen to His words. They knew that He was different from other men, and that His teaching was from God. But they were also attracted by His meekness and His kindness toward everyone.

He loved the poor and was eager to teach those who needed instruction. He healed the sick and was merciful to sinners. He said, "Come to Me, all you who labor and are burdened, and I will give you rest. Take My yoke upon you, and learn from Me, for I am meek and humble of heart; and you will find rest for your souls. For My yoke is easy, and My burden, light."

The great holiness of His life could be seen by everyone. Even His enemies were never able to prove that He had committed the slightest sin. Because He was holy, the pure of heart loved to be near Him, while sinners were turned from their wickedness and came to Him for forgiveness.

Of course, many people came to Him because they were curious to see Him perform miracles. But often they, too, received the grace to love Him and to follow Him.

Christ Has Mercy on Sinners

"Behold the Lamb of God! Behold the One who takes away the sins of the world!" With these words, John the Baptist introduced our blessed Savior to the people.

Recall what happened in the days of Moses: The Paschal lamb was sacrificed so that its blood, being sprinkled on the doorposts, would save the firstborn of the Israelites from death the night before they left Egypt. That event was a foreshadowing of Christ's sacrifice on the Cross. He was sacrificed so that His blood would save those who believe in Him from the death of sin.

The sacrifices of the Old Law could not open the gates of heaven, for only God Himself could take away the sins of the world. By His death on the cross, Christ paid the debt that the human race owed to God and bought for us the right to enter the kingdom of heaven. God's will is that we should be made holy by the sacrifice of Jesus Christ.

Because Christ came to save sinners, He didn't shun them; He reached out to them. But the Pharisees criticized Him for associating with sinful people.

They were scandalized when He permitted a notoriously sinful woman to kiss His feet. They were shocked when He dined in the house of the tax collector. Whenever sinners drew close to Him to listen to Him, the Pharisees murmured, saying, "This man receives sinners and even eats with them."

Jesus said to His critics: "Which of you who has a hundred sheep, and loses one of them, won't leave the ninety-nine in the wilderness and go after the one that's lost until you find it? And when you've found it, you carry it on your shoulders with joy; you come home, call together your friends and neighbors, saying to them, 'Rejoice with me, because I've found my sheep that was lost!'

"I say to you that in the same way, there will be joy in heaven over even one sinner who repents, more than over ninety-nine righteous ones who need no repentance.

"Or what woman, having ten coins, but losing one of them, doesn't light a candle and sweep the house and search carefully until she finds it? And when she's found it, she calls together her friends and neighbors, saying, 'Rejoice with me, because I've found the coin that I had lost.' I say to you, in the same way there will be joy among the angels of God over one sinner repenting."

The Wayward Son

Then our Savior told them this beautiful story:

"A certain man had two sons. The younger of them said to his father, 'Father, go ahead and give me now my share of your property.' So the father divided his property and gave the son the portion that he would one day have inherited. Not many days later, the younger son gathered up all his wealth and journeyed into a faraway country.

"There he squandered his fortune by living a wild and wicked life. After he had spent everything he had, there came a terrible famine in that country, and he began to be in need. So he went and hired himself out to one of the citizens there, who sent him to his farm to feed the pigs. He was so hungry that he would gladly have eaten the slop that the pigs were eating, but no one would let him have even that.

"At last he came to his senses. He said to himself, 'How many hired men in my father's estate have an abundance of bread, while I'm perishing here with hunger! I'll get up and go to my father, and say to him: Father, I have sinned against heaven and against you. I'm no longer worthy to be called your son. Make me one of your hired servants.'

"Getting up, he went home to his father. When he was still a long way off, his father saw him and was moved with compassion. Running to meet him, he kissed him on his neck.

"The son said, 'Father, I have sinned against heaven and against you. I'm not worthy to be called your son.'

"But the father said to his servants, 'Hurry and bring out the best robe and put it on him, and put a ring on his finger, and sandals on his feet. Then bring out the fattened calf—the one we've long been preparing for a grand feast—and kill it, so that we can eat and celebrate. Because this, my son, was dead, and has come to life again; he was lost, and now is found.' And they began to celebrate.

"Now his elder son was in the field. When he came near the house, he heard music and dancing. So he called one of the servants and asked what this meant. The servant said to him, 'Your brother has come home, and your father has killed the fattened calf, because he's gotten him back safe.'

"Hearing this, the elder son became angry and refused to go into the house. So his father came out and began urging him to come in. But the elder brother said to his father, 'Look! For all these many years I've been serving you, and I've never disobeyed you. Yet you've never given me even as much as a little goat to have a party with my friends! But as soon as this son has come home—the one who has squandered his fortune in sinful living—you've killed the fattened calf for him.'

"But his father said to him, 'Son, you are always with me, and all I have is yours. But we had to celebrate and rejoice, for this brother of yours was dead, and has come to life again; he was lost, and now is found.'"

This powerful story of forgiveness should remind us that God's mercy has no end. Even if we have committed serious sins, He waits for us to repent and come to the Sacrament of Reconciliation so that we can be forgiven and start over.

The Laborers in the Vineyard

Our Savior told yet another story so sinners can know that God is always ready to welcome them when they repent. It's never too late to return to Him.

"The kingdom of heaven," Jesus said, "is like the owner of an estate who went out early in the morning to hire laborers for his vineyard. And having agreed with the laborers to pay them one denarius a day, he sent them into his vineyard.

"Going out again about nine in the morning, he saw others standing around in the marketplace needing work. He said to them, 'You go into my vineyard, too, and I'll give you a just wage.' So they went to work in the vineyard.

"Again he went out about noon and three in the afternoon, and did the same thing. Then finally, about five in the afternoon he went out and found others standing around. He said to them, 'Why are you standing here all day doing nothing?'

"They said to him, 'Because no one has hired us.'

"So he said to them, 'You go work in my vineyard, too.'

"When evening had come, the owner of the vineyard said to his steward, 'Call the laborers and pay them their wages, beginning with the last ones hired, and ending with the first.'

"When those came forward who hadn't started to work until five in the afternoon, each of them received a denarius. And when the first to be hired came in their turn, they expected to receive more. But each of them also received a denarius.

"Once they were paid, they began to complain to the owner of the estate, saying, 'These last laborers to come worked only one hour, yet you've paid them as much as you've paid us—even though we're the ones who had to carry the greatest burden of the work, all in the heat of the day.'

"But the owner said to one of them, 'Friend, I'm doing you no wrong. Didn't you agree with me to be paid a denarius? Take what's yours and go. It's my choice whether I'll give the same wages to all of you."

In a similar way, God offers mercy to sinners. Both those who repent late in life and those who have served Him all their life can enjoy together the reward of eternal happiness in heaven.

The Woman Caught in Adultery

What Jesus taught about God's mercy He also practiced in His dealings with people who had seriously sinned.

Early one morning, He came into the Temple. Some scribes and Pharisees came up to Him, bringing with them a woman. They said to Him, "Teacher, this woman has been caught in the act of adultery. Now, Moses and the law commanded us to stone to death such a sinner. But what do you say?"

This question was intended to entrap our blessed Savior. If He told them to follow the Law of Moses and put the woman to death, they would say that He didn't love sinners and showed no mercy. If He told them to set her free, they could accuse Him before the high priest of contradicting the Law.

Jesus at first said nothing. Instead, stooping down, He began to write with His finger in the dust.

They watched Him for a minute, then they repeated their question. Standing up, He said to them: "Whoever among you is without sin, let him cast the first stone at her." Then, stooping down again, He continued to write on the ground.

Hearing this, the scribes and Pharisees began to slip away, one by one, beginning with the eldest. Finally, only Jesus and the woman remained.

Then Jesus stood up again and said to her, "Woman, where are your accusers? Has no one condemned you?"

She answered, "No one, Lord."

Then Jesus said, "Neither will I condemn you. Go your way, and from now on, sin no more."

The Cost of Discipleship

Many of those who listened to Jesus were attracted by His doctrine and felt in their hearts a desire to follow Him. But they also loved the things of this world and didn't have the courage to give them up.

One day, one of the scribes came to Jesus and said, "Teacher, I will follow you wherever you go." But Jesus wanted him to know how difficult it would be to follow Him, so He warned him: "The foxes have holes, and the birds of the air have nests. But the Son of Man has no place to lay His head." Jesus was speaking of Himself, because *the Son of Man* was one of the titles given to the Messiah.

One of His disciples said, "I will follow You, Lord, but first let me go and say goodbye to everyone at home."

Perhaps Jesus knew that the man's family would try to talk him out of following Him. He said to him, "No one who puts his hand to the plow yet looks back is fit for the kingdom of God." Our Lord realized that the new life the disciple wanted to begin was so different from his previous way of life, he couldn't afford to keep looking back wistfully at the way things were before.

"Whoever is not with Me, is against Me," said the Savior. "Whoever doesn't gather with Me, scatters. No one can serve two masters: Either He will hate the one and love the other, or he will be devoted to one and despise the other. You cannot serve both God and money."

Jesus and Nicodemus

One wealthy man who may have had to struggle with Jesus' teaching about riches was a Pharisee who lived in Jerusalem, a member of the Sanhedrin named Nicodemus. Soon after Our Lord began His public life, He went up to Jerusalem to celebrate the Feast of the Passover. While there, He preached to the people and performed miracles.

When the news about Jesus reached Nicodemus, he made up his mind to go and see Him so he could find out whether or not He truly was the Messiah. Not wishing the other Pharisees and the members of the Sanhedrin to know about his visit, he came during the night, under cover of darkness. He said to Jesus, "Rabbi, we know that you have come as a teacher from God. For no one could do the things you do unless God were with him."

That night, Our Lord instructed Nicodemus and answered all his questions. He told him how God loved the world so much that He gave His only divine Son, so that whoever would believe in Him would not perish, but have everlasting life. Jesus foretold that as the Son of God, He Himself would one day be lifted up, just as the serpent had been lifted up by Moses in the desert. All who would look to Him in faith could be saved.

Jesus also told Nicodemus of the new life of grace found in the Sacrament of Baptism. "Truly, truly, I say to you," said the Savior, "unless a man is born again of water and the Holy Spirit, he cannot enter the kingdom of heaven."

Nicodemus admired Jesus and His teachings. But at this time he didn't have the courage to follow Him openly, because most of his fellow Pharisees were opposed to Jesus. The day would come, however, when Nicodemus would show his commitment to Our Lord boldly, without regard for what others thought of him.

Mary Magdalene and Mary of Bethany

One of the open followers of Jesus was Mary Magdalene, from the town of Magdala on the Sea of Galilee. Our Lord delivered Mary Magdalene from seven demons who had tormented her, and she remained grateful to Him all her life. She appears frequently in the Gospel accounts, since she traveled with Jesus and served Him as a member of His band of disciples. She was especially close to Him in His death and resurrection.

In addition to Mary Magdalene and Mary the mother of Jesus, there was another woman named Mary who believed in Our Lord and became friends with Him. She lived with her sister, Martha, and her brother, Lazarus, in a village called Bethany, not far from Jerusalem. Once when Jesus was on His way to Jerusalem, He stopped at their home.

The three greeted Him joyfully, and Mary sat at His feet, listening to every word that He spoke. Meanwhile, Martha was busy preparing a meal for Jesus. Seeing Mary sitting at the feet of the Savior, she complained to Him: "Lord, is it no concern to You that my sister has left me to serve alone? So tell her to help me!"

Jesus replied: "Martha, Martha, you are anxious and troubled about many things. But only one thing is necessary. Mary has chosen the best part, and it will not be taken away from her."

Jesus wasn't saying that Martha's service to Him and the others was unimportant. He wanted to remind her that her busyness shouldn't keep her from making her relationship to Jesus her top priority.

Jesus and the Penitent Woman

Another woman who encountered Jesus also came to Him when He was a guest in someone's home. One day a Pharisee named Simon invited Jesus to dine with him. While He was there, a woman came into the room where they were eating.

She fell on her knees at the feet of the Savior. Filled with sorrow for her sins, she wept bitterly. She bathed His feet with her tears and wiped them dry with her hair. Then she kissed His feet and anointed them with some precious ointment that she had brought with her.

When Simon saw this, he said to himself, "If this man were a prophet, He would surely know what kind of woman this is who is touching Him, and that she is a sinner."

Jesus, reading his thoughts, said to him, "Simon, I have something to say to you."

The Pharisee replied, "Teacher, what is it?"

Jesus said, "A certain creditor had two debtors. One owed him five hundred denarii; the other, fifty. Since they had no means of paying the debts, he forgave them both. So which of them will love him more?"

Simon answered, "I suppose the one to whom he forgave more."

Jesus said, "You have judged rightly." Then, turning to the woman, he said to Simon, "Do you see this woman?

"I came into your house, and you gave Me no water to wash My feet. But she has bathed My feet with her tears and wiped them with her hair.

"You gave Me no kiss to greet Me. But she, from the moment she entered the room, has not stopped kissing My feet.

"You didn't anoint My head with oil. But she has anointed My feet with ointment.

"For this reason, I say to you, her sins, which are many, are forgiven, because she has loved much. But he who is forgiven little, loves little."

Then He said to the woman, "Your sins are forgiven."

All those at the meal began to say among themselves, "Who is this man, who even forgives sins?"

But Jesus said to the woman, "Your faith has saved you. Go in peace."

Jesus and Zacchaeus

Our Lord's gentleness toward those who were despised is shown by the way He treated Zacchaeus. This man was hated by the people because he was the chief collector of taxes in Jericho. On His last journey to Jerusalem, just before His passion and death, Jesus passed through Jericho, where Zacchaeus lived.

Zacchaeus wanted to see Jesus. But he was so short, he couldn't see over the heads of the people in the crowd standing around him. So Zacchaeus climbed up into the branches of a nearby sycamore tree to see Jesus as He passed by.

Coming to the tree, Jesus looked up and saw Zacchaeus. "Hurry and come down," He said to him, "for I must stay at your house today."

Zacchaeus climbed down from the tree in a hurry and received Jesus in his home with great joy. When the crowd saw this, they murmured against Jesus, because He chose to be the guest of a man they considered a sinner. But Zacchaeus said, "Lord, I give half of my possessions to the poor. And if I have defrauded anyone of anything, I give back to him four times as much."

Jesus said to him, "This day salvation has come to this house. . . . For the Son of Man came to seek and save what was lost."

The Woman at the Well

One day, Jesus and His apostles were passing through Samaria, the land that lies between Galilee and Judea.

As we noted before, the Jews and the Samaritans usually kept their distance from each other. In fact, most Jews refused even to walk through Samaria; instead, they would take a long route around just to avoid having to do with Samaritans. But Jesus came to earth to be the Savior of everyone, so He didn't avoid Samaria as so many others did.

One day He and His apostles came to a city that was called Sychar. Outside the town was a well that had been dug by Jacob, Abraham's grandson. It was late in the afternoon, and that day they had journeyed far. So Jesus was tired, and He sat beside the well to rest while His apostles went into the city to buy food.

While Jesus was sitting there, a Samaritan woman came to draw water from the well. Jesus asked her for a drink.

The woman was quite surprised that this Jewish stranger would speak to her. "How is it that You," she asked, "even though You're a Jew, ask a Samaritan woman for a drink? For the Jews have nothing to do with the Samaritans." In fact, Jews usually refused even to drink out of a cup that had been used by a Samaritan!

Jesus didn't take offense at this answer. Instead, He said to her kindly, "If you knew the gift of God and who it is that asks you for a drink, you might have asked Him, and He would have given you living water."

The woman was puzzled by His words. "Sir," she said, "You have nothing to draw water with, and the well is deep. Where do You get this living water? Are You greater than our father Jacob, who gave us the well, and drank from it himself, and his children, and his flocks?"

Jesus answered, "Whoever drinks this water will thirst again. But whoever drinks of the water that I will give him will never thirst. . . . The water that I will give him will become in him a fountain of waters springing up to eternal life."

Not surprisingly, the woman still wasn't quite sure what He meant. "Sir," she said, "give me this water, so that I won't get thirsty or have to come here to draw water."

"Go, call your husband to come here," said Jesus to her.

She replied, "I have no husband."

Jesus said to her, "You're right to say, 'I have no husband,' for you've had five husbands, and the one you now have is not your husband. You have answered truthfully."

The woman was startled. Jesus seemed to know the hidden secrets of her life! So she changed her tone and changed the subject. "Sir," she said, "I can see that You're a prophet. Now, our fathers worshipped here on Mount Gerizim; but You, being a Jew, say that Jerusalem is the place where we must worship."

Jesus said to her, "Woman, believe Me, the hour is coming when you'll worship the Father neither on this mountain nor in Jerusalem. You Samaritans worship what you don't know; we worship what we know. For salvation is from the Jews. But the hour is coming, and now is, when true worshippers will worship the Father in spirit and in truth. . . . God is spirit, and those who worship Him must worship Him in spirit and in truth."

The woman said, "I know that the Messiah is coming, and when He comes, He'll tell us everything."

Jesus said to her, "I *am* the Messiah—the One you're talking to right now."

Some Samaritans Believe in Christ

By this time the apostles had made their purchases in the town. Returning to Jesus, they were surprised to see Him talking to a Samaritan woman. But the woman left her water jar standing at the well and hurried back to the city.

There, she began telling everyone: "Come, see a Man who has told me everything I've ever done. Can He be the Christ?" Soon a large crowd of Samaritans were on their way out to the well to see Jesus for themselves.

Meanwhile, the apostles had set out the food they had purchased and urged Jesus, "Rabbi, eat."

He answered, "I have food to eat that you don't know about." The disciples looked at one another and said, "Did someone already bring Him something to eat?"

But Jesus said, "My food is to do the will of the One who sent Me."

In the distance they could see a crowd of Samaritans coming out of the city, their white clothes gleaming in the afternoon sun like a field of ripened barley grain. Pointing to them, Jesus said, "Don't you say, 'There are yet four months before the harvest'? Well, I say to you, look up and see the fields. They are already white for the harvest."

The Samaritans came to Jesus at the well, and He spoke to them about the kingdom of heaven. They begged Him to stay with them, and He stayed at Sychar two days.

Many of the Samaritans believed in Him because the woman had told them that He knew everything that she had done. But many more believed in Him because of His own words. They said to the woman, "We no longer believe simply because of what you said, for now we have heard Him for ourselves, and we know that He is in truth the Savior of the world."

This fascinating story reminds us how much we need Christ, who is the "living water" bringing us eternal life. But it also has much to teach us about sharing our faith through Our Lord's example. He wasn't afraid to cross social and religious boundaries to talk about the good news of God's kingdom. And though He spoke with great patience and charity, He wasn't afraid to challenge other people's thinking and their way of life.

CHAPTER 5

Christ, the Great Teacher

Jesus Teaches the People

The Son of God became Man in order to take upon Himself the sins of the world and to suffer and die for us on the Cross. But in order for us to profit by His sacrifice, He had to teach us how to live a holy life. Otherwise, through ignorance we would fall back into our sins.

This is why Jesus spent the three years of His public life preaching to the people and telling them what they must do to enter the kingdom of heaven. Many people listened to Him and admired His teaching, because He taught them as Someone who had power and authority—not as the scribes and Pharisees taught.

The Messiah had no one place to preach. Instead, He went among the people and spoke to them wherever He found them. He taught in the fields, in the streets of the town, in the courts of the Temple, and even from the boat of Simon Peter.

One of His sermons is known as *the Sermon on the Mount,* because it was preached on the side of a small mountain or hill. We can imagine our Savior seated on a rock, high on the side of the hill, with the people gathered together below Him, some of them sitting on the ground, and some of them standing up.

It was in this sermon that Jesus gave us the eight *Beatitudes,* which tell us the actions and attitudes that God blesses. The sermon offers us what might be called the laws of the kingdom of heaven that Christ came to establish on earth. Jesus said:

> "Blessed are the poor in spirit, for theirs is the kingdom of heaven.
> "Blessed are the meek, for they will possess the earth.
> "Blessed are those who mourn, for they will be comforted.
> "Blessed are those who hunger and thirst for justice, for they will be satisfied.
> "Blessed are the merciful, for they will obtain mercy.
> "Blessed are the pure in heart, for they will see God.
> "Blessed are the peacemakers, for they will be called children of God.
> "Blessed are those who suffer persecution for the sake of justice, for theirs is the kingdom of heaven.
> "Blessed are you when men reproach you, and persecute you, and—speaking falsely—say all kinds of evil against you, for My sake. Be glad and rejoice, for your reward is great in heaven."

Jesus Himself was the perfect example of each of these beatitudes. For this reason, not only every word, but also every action of Christ is a lesson for us. That's why He said of Himself, "I am the way, the truth, and the life."

Jesus Teaches About Prayer

Christ showed us, for example, how necessary it is to refresh and strengthen our souls by frequent conversations with God. From time to time, our Savior left the people and went alone to the solitude of some mountain to pray. Often the Gospel tells us how He spent the whole night in prayer.

Once, after Jesus had spent the night in prayer, some of His disciples came to Him and said, "Lord, teach us how to pray."

Then Jesus gave them the following beautiful instructions: "When you are praying," He said, "don't multiply your words, as the Gentiles do. For they think that by saying a great deal, they will be heard. So don't be like them, for your Father knows what you need before you ask Him. In this manner, then, you must pray:

"Our Father, who art in heaven, hallowed be Thy name; Thy kingdom come; Thy will be done on earth as it is in heaven. Give us this day our daily bread; and forgive us our trespasses, as we forgive those who trespass against us; and lead us not into temptation, but deliver us from evil."

Then Jesus continued: "Imagine that you have a friend, and you go to him at midnight and say, 'Friend, lend me three loaves of bread, because another friend of mine has come to me on a journey, and I have nothing to feed him.'

"Perhaps your friend might call out from inside the house: 'Don't disturb me! The house is locked up for the night, and my children are in bed. I can't get up and get bread for you!'

"But I tell you: If you continue knocking, even if your

friend wouldn't get up to help you because he's your friend, just because of your persistence he'll get up and give you as much as you need.

"So I say to you, ask, and it will be given to you; seek, and you will find; knock, and it will be opened to you. For everyone who asks, receives; and the one who seeks, finds; and to the one who knocks, it will be opened.

"If one of you asks his father for bread, will he hand him a stone? Or if you ask him for a fish, will he hand you a snake? If you, sinful as you are, know how to give good gifts to your children, how much more will your heavenly Father give good things to those who ask Him?"

With these and other encouragements, Jesus called the people to place their trust in God as their heavenly Father who loved them and cared for them.

The Kingdom of Heaven Is Announced

Our divine Savior spoke constantly of the kingdom of heaven. He began His public preaching by repeating the message of John the Baptist, "Repent, for the kingdom of heaven is at hand!" Many of the people thought that He intended to lead a great revolt against the Romans, drive them out, and win back for Himself the throne of David, His ancestor.

But Jesus was not thinking of an earthly kingdom. He was thinking of the time when all people would know that they belonged to God and that they were put here on earth to do His holy will. God didn't create us for this world, yet Jesus saw how many people were living as though money, or pleasure, or earthly power were the only thing that mattered.

Jesus was a wonderful teacher and knew how to present His doctrine in such a clear way that His listeners would have no difficulty in understanding it. Frequently He spoke to them in *parables*—that is to say, He compared the things of God to things from their everyday life. If He saw a farmer sowing seed in his field, for example, or a fisherman pulling his net out of the sea, or a shepherd watching his sheep, or a father and mother taking care of their children, He would make use of the fact to point out some lesson about the kingdom of heaven. Often, too, the parable was a story He made up to help them understand some difficult doctrine.

In the sermon that He preached from the mountainside our Savior said: "Don't lay up for yourselves treasures on earth, where rust and moth consume, and where thieves break in and steal. But lay up for yourselves treasures in heaven, where neither rust nor moth consumes, nor thieves break in and steal. For where your treasure is, there also will be your heart.

"Don't be anxious about your life," Jesus said, "what you will eat, nor about your body, what you will put on. Isn't life a greater thing than food, and the body greater than clothing?

"Look at the birds of the air: They don't sow crops, or reap them, or gather them into barns. Yet your heavenly Father feeds them. Aren't you of much more value than they are? Which one of you by worrying can add even a little time to your life on earth?

"And as for clothing, why are you anxious? Consider how the lilies of the field grow. They don't work or spin thread for cloth. But I say to you that not even Solomon in all his glory was clothed like one of these. And if God clothes the grass of the field this way, which flourishes today, but tomorrow is burned for fuel, how much more will He clothe you? You of little faith!

"So don't be anxious, saying, 'What will we eat?' or 'What will we drink?' or 'What will we wear?' These are all the things Gentiles seek. For your Father knows that

you need these things. So seek first the kingdom of God and His justice, and all these things will be given to you besides."

Jesus Teaches Love

Worrying about the future wasn't the only problem in the spiritual life of the people. They also failed to love God and one another as the Law had commanded them.

In the Book of Deuteronomy, Moses said, "Love the Lord your God with all your heart, and with all your soul, and with all your strength." In the Book of Leviticus we read, "Love your neighbor as yourself." The people had forgotten the meaning of these two commandments in the Law of Moses. Many of them loved themselves more than they loved God, and because they loved themselves, they loved only those who were friendly to them and did them favors.

Jesus didn't come to destroy the Law of Moses, but to explain it to the people and show them how to obey it as perfectly as possible. He told them:

"You have heard that it was said to those long ago, 'Love your neighbor and hate your enemy.' But I say to you, love your enemies, do good to those who hate you. Bless those who curse you, pray for those who speak evil of you.

"In this way you will prove yourselves children of your Father in heaven. For He makes His sun to rise on those who are evil as well as those who are good. And He sends rain on both those who are righteous and those who are unrighteous.

"If you love only those who love you, what reward will you have? Don't even the tax collectors do that much? If you greet your brothers only, you're doing no more than the unbelievers . . . So be merciful, then, as your heavenly Father is merciful."

Jesus Teaches Forgiveness

One day, Simon Peter asked our Savior, "How often must I forgive my brother who sins against me? Seven times?"

Jesus answered, "Not seven times, but seventy times seven times.

"For the kingdom of heaven is like a king who wanted to settle accounts with his servants. When he had begun the settlement, one was brought to him who owed him ten thousand talents. Since the servant had no money to pay what he owed, the king commanded that he and his wife and his children must be sold, along with all that he owned, in order to pay his debt.

"But the servant fell down and begged him for mercy, saying, 'Have patience with me, and I will pay you everything I owe.' Moved with compassion, the king let him go and canceled the debt.

"But as that servant went out, he found one of his fellow servants who owed him only a hundred denarii. Seizing him by the throat, he demanded, 'Pay me what you owe!'

"So his fellow servant fell down and began to beg him, saying, 'Have patience with me, and I will pay you everything I owe.' But he refused. Instead, he had him cast into prison.

"Now his fellow servants, seeing what had happened, were greatly distressed. So they came and informed their lord of what had taken place. Then the king called him and said, 'You wicked servant! I forgave you all your debt because you begged me. Shouldn't you also, then, have had mercy on your fellow servant, just as I had mercy on you?'

"Then in anger the king delivered him to the torturers until he paid all the debt. So also will My heavenly Father do to you, if you don't each forgive your brothers from your hearts."

Jesus Forbids Retaliation and Judging

Jesus taught other important lessons as well about how we must treat others. According to the Law of Moses, a man who was injured might seek retaliation in certain cases. But the law of love, which our Savior preached, permitted no revenge.

Jesus told the people: "You have heard it said, 'Take an eye for an eye, and a tooth for a tooth.' But I say to you, don't resist the evildoer. On the contrary, if someone strikes you on your right cheek, turn to him the other cheek. And if someone goes to court to take away your coat, let him have your cloak as well."

In the Sermon on the Mount, our blessed Lord said, "Don't judge, so that you won't be judged. Don't condemn, so that you won't be condemned. Forgive, and you will be forgiven.

"Give, and it will be given to you. Good measure, pressed down, shaken together, running over, they will pour it into your lap. For with the same measure with which you measure, it will be measured to you.

"Why do you see the speck in your brother's eye, when you don't consider the beam that's in your own eye? Or how can you say to your brother, 'Let me pull the speck out of your eye,' when you yourself can't see the beam in your own eye? Hypocrite! First pull the beam out of your own eye, and then you'll see clearly enough to pull out the speck in your brother's eye."

One sentence spoken by our blessed Savior sums up the whole law of love. We call it the Golden Rule. It says, "All that you want others to do to you, do also to them, for this is the Law and the prophets."

Jesus Teaches About the Family

Jesus taught about family life as well. According to the Law of Moses, it was lawful for a married couple to get a divorce for certain reasons. Knowing that Jesus condemned divorce, the Pharisees came to Him one day and asked, "Is it lawful to divorce for any cause?"

By this question they hoped to entrap Him. If Jesus said that it wasn't lawful, they could say that He was teaching doctrines contrary to the Law of Moses.

Knowing what was in their minds, Jesus replied with

a quote from Scripture: "Haven't you read that the Creator, from the beginning, made them male and female, and said, 'For this reason a man will leave his father and mother and be joined to his wife, and the two will become one'? So they are no longer two but one. What God has joined together, then, let no one tear apart."

The Pharisees answered: "Why then did Moses command that a man must give a certificate of divorce if he wanted to put his wife away?"

Jesus replied: "Because of the hardness of your hearts, Moses gave permission. But in the beginning it wasn't that way."

Jesus knew that home is the place where we first learn how to love one another. Children are happy when their parents love them. They see how happy their parents are because they love each other. Because Jesus wanted all children to have happy homes, He taught that married couples should not divorce. Love should bind a family together for a lifetime.

The Good Samaritan

Our Lord knew that love must be the guiding principle, not only in the family, but in our relationships with everyone. So He told a parable one day to emphasize that truth and to explain it in a practical way.

While Jesus was preaching, one of the scribes stood up and interrupted him with a question. "Teacher," he said, "what must I do to gain eternal life?" The man was not sincere. He was simply testing Jesus to see what He would say.

Knowing this, Jesus said to him, "What is written in the Law? What do you read there?"

The scribe answered, "You will love the Lord your God with your whole heart, and with your whole soul, and with your whole strength, and with your whole mind; and you shall love your neighbor as you love yourself."

"You have answered rightly," said Jesus. "Do this, and you will live."

But the scribe wasn't satisfied with that answer. He pressed further. "Well, then," he said, "who *is* my neighbor?" Then Jesus replied with this parable:

"A certain man was going down from Jerusalem to Jericho, and he fell among robbers. They stripped him and beat him and went their way, leaving him half dead.

"But as it happened, a certain priest was going down the same way. Seeing the wounded man, the priest passed him by. In the same way a Levite, when he was near the place and saw him, also passed him by. But a certain Samaritan came nearby on his journey."

You can imagine at this point what the people were thinking as they listened to Jesus. After all, the Jews usually treated Samaritans with contempt. If even a priest and a Levite refused to help the man, what would they expect of a Samaritan? But the parable had a surprise ending.

Jesus continued: "And when the Samaritan saw the wounded man, he was moved with compassion. Going up to him, he bound up his wounds, pouring oil and wine on them to cleanse them and help them to heal. Then he set the wounded man on his own animal to ride, brought him to an inn, and took care of him.

"The next day the Samaritan took out two denarii and gave them to the innkeeper, saying, 'Take care of him, and whatever more you spend, I will repay you on my way back.'"

Then Jesus asked the scribe: "Which of these three, in your opinion, proved himself a neighbor to the one who fell among the robbers?"

The scribe answered, "The one who showed mercy to him."

Jesus said to him, "Go and do the same."

The Foolishness of Living for This World

In order to show the people how foolish it is to live for this world and its pleasures, Jesus told them this story:

"There was a certain rich man who used to clothe himself in costly purple cloth and fine linen, and who feasted every day in splendid fashion. And there was a certain poor man, named Lazarus, who lay at his gate, covered with sores. He longed to be filled even with the crumbs that fell from the rich man's table . . .

"Now it happened that the poor man died and was carried away by the angels into Abraham's bosom"—that is, the place of rest after death for those who are faithful. "And the rich man also died. And in hell, being in torment, he looked up and saw Abraham far away, and Lazarus with him.

"So he cried out, 'Father Abraham, have pity on me, and send Lazarus to dip the tip of his finger in water to cool my tongue. I'm tormented in this flame!'

"But Abraham said to him, 'Son, remember that in your lifetime, you received good things, while Lazarus endured evil things. But now, he's comforted while you're tormented. Besides all that, between us and you a great chasm has been fixed, so that those who want to pass over from this side to yours cannot, and they cannot cross from your side to ours.'

"Then the rich man said, 'Father, I beg you, send Lazarus to my father's house. For I have five brothers, and he must warn them so that they too won't come to this place of torment.'

"Abraham said to him, 'They have Moses and the prophets. Let your brothers listen to them.'

"But the rich man said, 'No, Father Abraham, but if someone goes to them from the dead, they'll repent.'

"Abraham said to him, 'If they won't listen to Moses

and the prophets, they won't believe even if someone rises from the dead.'"

With this parable, Jesus was warning us against neglecting those who are in need. But He was also warning that some of those who heard His message would refuse to believe in Him, even after He had proved that He was God's Son by rising from the dead.

CHAPTER 6

Christ Works Miracles

The Wedding Feast at Cana

The people flocked to Jesus to hear His gracious teaching. But how could they know that He was truly speaking for God? The miracles He performed were the evidence God provided to show that Jesus was His divine Son, in whom He was well pleased.

The first of those miracles took place at the very beginning of His public life. Jesus didn't hold himself aloof from the people, but was always ready to take part in their innocent pleasures. So He was pleased to accept an invitation to attend a wedding feast at Cana, in Galilee.

Mary, His mother, was also invited. Taking with Him His first disciples, Jesus left the Jordan and made the long journey into Galilee, so He could attend the feast.

During the festivities, Mary noticed that the servants were greatly worried. She asked them what was the matter, and they told her that the wine had run out. So Mary came to Jesus and said, "They have no wine."

Jesus answered, "What would you have me do? . . . My hour has not yet come."

But Mary knew that Jesus loved these people, and He wanted them to be happy on their wedding day. Running out of wine for the guests would be an embarrassment. So she said to the waiters, "Do whatever He tells you."

Six large stone water jars were standing nearby. Jesus said to the waiters, "Fill the jars with water." They filled them to the brim.

Then He said, "Draw some out, now, and take it to the chief steward of the feast." They did as He commanded. The water had been changed into wine, and when the chief steward tasted it, he found it much better than the wine he had already been serving.

He didn't know where it came from, and he thought that the bridegroom had made a mistake in serving the best wine last. So he called him and said, "Every man at first sets out the good wine, and when the guests have drunk freely, then the wine of lesser quality. But you've kept the good wine until now."

This was the first miracle that Jesus worked. He performed it at the request of His blessed Mother, so that these friends of His could celebrate their wedding day without embarrassment.

The Barren Fig Tree

One day Jesus and His apostles were on their way from Bethany to Jerusalem. As they went along, Jesus became hungry. Seeing a fig tree in the distance, He went up to it to find out whether there might be any fruit. Though it was covered with leaves, there were no figs on it.

Then Jesus said to the fig tree, "May no one eat fruit from you ever again." And His disciples heard what He had said.

They went on into the city to spend the day, and that evening, they returned to Bethany. On the following morning, they passed the fig tree again on their way back to Jerusalem. It had shriveled from the roots up.

Peter remembered what had happened the day before, so he said, "Rabbi, look! The fig tree you cursed has withered up."

Jesus wanted Peter and the others to know that the same divine power that had miraculously withered the fig tree could also work on their behalf, if they had faith. So He told them: "Have faith in God. Truly, I tell you, you can say to this mountain, 'Get up and throw yourself into the sea!' And if you believe in your heart, without wavering, that what you say will be done, it will indeed be done for you."

Jesus and the Apostles Seek a Place of Rest

Once the people became familiar with Our Lord's teaching and miracles, they came to hold Him in great admiration. They were always crowding around Him, and they gave Him little chance to rest. No wonder, then, that sometimes Jesus was exhausted.

When the apostles returned from their first missionary journey, they found the Savior worn out. They, too, were weary and footsore. Many people seeking Jesus' ministry were coming and going, and the apostles couldn't find time even to eat.

To make matters worse, their hearts were filled with grief because they had just heard about the death of John the Baptist. So Jesus said, "Come away with me by yourselves into a place of solitude, and rest awhile."

Nearby was the Sea of Galilee. The apostles found a boat and set sail for the northern shore, with our blessed Savior aboard as well. There they knew they would find a lonely wilderness area where, far from the cities and the crowds, they could rest their bodies and refresh their souls.

But in spite of all their precautions, someone had seen them sail away. Then, too, the winds were against them, and it took them much longer to sail across the water than they had expected. News of their departure had spread among the people. So they followed Jesus, some by boat and some by walking around to the other shore.

When the ship reached the shore, Jesus and the apostles found a great number of people waiting for them. Walking on through the crowd, they went on into the wilderness. Soon they came to a grass-covered hill, and they sat down on the ground to rest.

But there was to be no rest for them that day. The crowds followed after them, and soon they were surrounded by about five thousand people.

Jesus felt compassion for the crowds. He couldn't send them away, because they were like sheep without a shepherd, and they had come to Him to learn about the love of God. So He laid aside His own weariness. He taught them all day long about the kingdom of God, and He healed all their sick.

Jesus Multiplies the Loaves and Fishes

When the day was almost done, the shadows of the evening began to close in on them. The apostles came to Jesus and said, "This is a remote place, and the hour is late. Send the people away, so they can go into the villages to buy food for themselves."

But Jesus replied, "They don't need to go away. Give them something to eat."

The apostles were skeptical. "Are we to go and buy two hundred denarii worth of bread, and give it to them to eat?"

Jesus asked, "How many loaves do you have? Go and see."

One of the apostles, Andrew, the brother of Simon Peter, said, "There's a boy here with five barley loaves and two fishes, but what are these among so many?"

Jesus said, "Have the people sit down on the grass in groups of fifty." The apostles did as Jesus instructed, and soon that great multitude was sitting down on the green grass.

Then Jesus took the five loaves and the two fishes. Looking up to heaven, He blessed the loaves, broke them, and distributed them to His apostles to give out to the multitude, along with the fish.

The people were very hungry. Many of them had left home the night before, and they had been listening to Jesus all day long. So they all ate as much as they wanted, until they were satisfied.

Then Jesus said to His apostles, "Gather up the fragments that are left over, so that nothing will be lost." So they gathered them up, and they filled twelve baskets with the leftover pieces of the five barley loaves.

When the people saw the great miracle that Jesus had performed, they said, "This is truly the prophet who is to come into the world." Knowing that they had it in mind to take Him by force and make Him king, Jesus went away up the mountain by Himself. That was not the kind of kingdom He had come to establish.

Jesus Calms the Storm

One evening, after Jesus had spent the whole day healing the sick and teaching the people, He called His apostles together. Together with them He got into a little boat on the Sea of Galilee. He said to them, "Let's go over to the other side of the sea." Jesus was tired out from the labors of the day, so He fell asleep quickly.

They were about halfway across the water when suddenly a great storm arose. The wind blew, and soon great waves were dashing against the sides of the boat and onto the men inside. The boat took on so much water that it looked as if it would surely sink.

All the while, Jesus was sleeping peacefully. So the apostles woke Him up, saying, "Master, Master, save us, or we'll die!"

Jesus got up and rebuked the wind and the raging sea, saying, "Peace, be still!" Immediately the storm ended, and the waters became calm. Then Jesus said to the apostles, "Where is your faith?"

Trembling with fear and wonder, the apostles said to one another, "Who, then, is this, that He commands even the winds and the sea, and they obey Him?"

Peter Walks on the Water With Jesus

A short time after this, Jesus was preaching to the people on the eastern shore of the Sea of Galilee. In the evening, He dismissed the people and told the apostles to get into the boat and row back to Capernaum. Then He went up a mountain alone to pray.

The sea was rough, and the apostles had a hard time rowing the boat because the wind went against them. They were still far from shore in the early morning hours before dawn, when they suddenly saw someone coming toward them, walking on the water. They were terrified, crying out, "It's a ghost!"

But the figure walking on the water spoke to them, saying, "Take courage! It's Jesus; don't be afraid."

Peter said, "Lord, if it's really you, tell me to come to you on the water."

Jesus said to Peter, "Come on!"

Peter immediately got out of the boat and started to walk toward Jesus on the water. But when Peter saw how strong the winds were blowing, he began to be afraid. At once he felt himself sinking.

Peter cried out, "Lord, save me!"

So Jesus reached out His hand and caught him, saying, "You of little faith! Why did you doubt?"

When they got into the boat, the wind ceased. Then

those who were in the boat worshipped Jesus, saying, "Truly, You are the Son of God."

Our Lord's miracle had helped them to understand more clearly who He was, and to put their trust in Him. But God's plan of salvation was still in many ways a mystery to them. They had much yet to learn, and they would see and hear much that would require of them a firm faith in God.

CHAPTER 7

Christ, the Friend of the Sick

The Sick Come to Jesus for Healing

Some of the most beautiful miracles that Jesus performed were miracles of healing. These cures were signs of Our Lord's compassion for those who were afflicted, both in body and in soul. They gave great consolation to the people, showing them that God cared about them.

On one memorable evening, Jesus and His disciples were staying in Capernaum. After the sun had set, the townspeople brought to Him all who were ill or possessed by demons. In fact, the whole town had gathered together at the door. That night He healed many who were afflicted with various diseases, and He cast out many demons.

Imagine the scene that evening at Capernaum. We can see the pleading look in the eyes of the poor, suffering people as they are brought to Jesus. We can hear their relatives and friends begging Him to cure them.

One by one, they are brought to His feet, and as He

looks at them lovingly, He lays His hands upon them. Immediately they are cured. Those who have been lying on stretchers rise up and stand on their feet. The lame throw away their crutches. The blind open their eyes and see for the first time. And the poor creatures who have been tortured by demons are now at rest and find in their hearts a great peace.

This is just one episode of miracles that took place wherever Jesus went. As the Gospel sums it up: "He went around doing good."

The Faith of the Roman Centurion

Not long after Jesus preached the Sermon on the Mount, He was returning to Capernaum, followed by great crowds of people. In that city lived a centurion, the officer in command of the Roman soldiers quartered in that neighborhood. He had a servant who was dear to him, and who was sick and at the point of death.

Hearing that Jesus had come to town, the centurion sent some of the Jewish elders to ask Him to come and heal his servant. When they came to Jesus, they begged Him earnestly, saying, "He's worthy to have you do this for him. For he loves our people, and he built us our synagogue."

So Jesus went with them. When he was a short distance from the house, the centurion sent friends to Him with the message: "Lord, don't trouble Yourself. I'm not worthy to have You come under my roof; that's why I didn't think myself worthy to come to You to make the request on my own. But only say the word, and my servant will be healed.

"For I too am a man subject to authority, with soldiers under me. I say to one, 'Go,' and he goes, and to another, 'Come,' and he comes; and to my servant, 'Do this,' and he does it."

When Jesus heard this, He was amazed. It was surprising indeed that a Gentile, a soldier from pagan Rome, would understand so well the power and authority of the Savior. Turning to the crowds who followed Him, Jesus said, "Truly, I say to you, even in Israel I haven't found such great faith."

When the messengers returned to the house, they found that the servant who had been sick was now in good health.

Jesus Heals a Paralyzed Man

The news spread through Capernaum that Jesus was in the city and was staying at a certain house. Immediately the people stopped whatever they were doing and hurried there to see Him and listen to His teaching. Soon a great crowd gathered that filled the house and spilled out the door. Outside in the street were many more, who strained their ears to hear the Savior's voice and tried to see Him over the heads of those in front of them.

Several men came along who were carrying on a bed a man who was paralyzed. They tried to push their way through the crowd so they could enter the house and ask Jesus to heal him. But the people wouldn't make way for them.

Finally, they came up with a plan. They climbed up on the roof of the house, removed some tiles to make a hole in it, and lowered the bed with the sick man through the opening. In this way they were able to lay him down in front of Jesus.

Our Lord admired their faith and their perseverance. He said to the paralyzed man, "Son, your sins are forgiven."

Hearing this, some of the scribes and Pharisees who were sitting there were outraged, thinking to themselves,

"Why does this man speak like this? It's blasphemy! Who can forgive sins but God alone?"

Knowing their thoughts, Jesus said to them, "Why do you question in your hearts? Which is easier to say to the paralytic: 'Your sins are forgiven you,' or to say to him, 'Get up, pick up your bed, and walk'?

"But so that you can know that the Son of Man has power on earth to forgive sins"—then He turned and said to the paralyzed man—"I say to you, get up, pick up your bed, and go home." Immediately the man got up, picked up the bed where he had been lying, and carried it home, glorifying God as he walked along.

The crowds, seeing what had happened, were filled with amazement. They praised God, saying, "We've seen astounding things today!"

A Woman Is Healed by Touching Jesus' Clothes

Yet another resident of Capernaum who encountered Jesus' healing power was a woman who had suffered from a flow of blood that had lasted twelve years. She had consulted many physicians and had spent all her money trying to be cured. But instead of improving, her condition had only grown worse.

One day, the woman saw Jesus passing by. She had heard the reports about the people Jesus had healed. So she said to herself, "If I can just touch the hem of His clothes, I can be healed."

But there was a problem. A great crowd surrounded Jesus, so she couldn't get near enough to speak to Him. So she worked her way through the crowd and, once she was close enough, she reached out her hand and touched the hem of His clothes. Immediately she was healed of her sickness.

Jesus knew right away that healing power had flowed out of Him into someone else. So He turned around, looking at the crowd, and asked, "Who touched My clothing?"

The disciples were puzzled. They said, "You can see that the crowd is pressing all around You, yet You ask, 'Who touched Me?'"

But Jesus insisted. He looked around at the people nearby.

Trembling with fear, the woman came and knelt before Him, telling Him what she had done. Then Jesus said to her, "Daughter, your faith has healed you. Go in peace."

Jesus Heals the Blind Man

One day, Jesus was walking along the road that leads from Jericho to Jerusalem, with a great crowd following Him. A blind man sat by the roadside, begging, because he couldn't work to make a living. His name was Bartimaeus.

Hearing all the voices of the crowd, Bartimaeus called out to ask what was happening. They told him that Jesus of Nazareth was passing by. He knew that Jesus could work miracles of healing, so when he heard this, he began to cry out, "Jesus, Son of David, have mercy on me!"

Some of the people were annoyed by his cries and told him to be quiet. But he cried out even louder, "Son of David, have mercy on me!" Hearing his cry, Jesus stopped and said, "Tell him to come to Me."

So the people called the blind man and said to him, "Get up. Take heart! He's calling you." So Bartimaeus jumped up, threw off his cloak, and came to Jesus.

Our Lord asked him, "What do you want Me to do for you?"

Bartimaeus said, “Rabbi, let me receive my sight.”

Jesus replied, “Go your way. Your faith has healed you.” Immediately the blind man received his sight and joined the crowd that was following Jesus.

The Blind Man and the Pharisees

One Sabbath day when Jesus and His apostles were walking through the narrow streets of Jerusalem, they met a man who had been blind from birth. He sat by the street, calling out to the people who passed by and begging them for alms.

The apostles asked Our Lord, "Rabbi, who has sinned, this man or his parents, that he would be born blind?" They asked this because it was the common belief among the Jews at that time that sickness and disease were a direct punishment from God for some sin that had been committed.

Jesus answered, "Neither this man nor his parents have sinned. But he was born blind so that the power of God can be demonstrated in him. I must perform the works of the One who sent Me while it is still day. Night is coming, when no one can work. As long as I am in the world, I am the Light of the world."

Then Jesus stooped down and spat on the ground. He made mud with the dirt and the spittle, then spread the mud on the eyes of the blind man. Jesus said to him, "Go, wash in the Pool of Siloam." So the blind man went to the Pool of Siloam, washed his eyes, and came back seeing.

The neighbors of the man who had been blind began to question him, and he told them that a man named Jesus had healed him. Finally they decided to bring him to the Pharisees. They too asked him how he had received his sight.

He replied: "He put mud on my eyes, and I washed, and now I see." Most of the Pharisees opposed Jesus, so they were looking for reasons to condemn Him. Hearing what the man said, some of them criticized what Jesus had done.

"This man is not from God. He doesn't keep the Sabbath!" They were claiming that making mud and healing someone were forms of work, which was forbidden on the Sabbath.

But others asked, "How can a man who's a sinner work such miracles?" And they began to argue among themselves. They even tried to question the parents of the man who was healed, so they could find some way to condemn Jesus or to disbelieve their son's story.

At last they hit upon a scheme. They sent for the man who had been blind and said to him, "Give glory to God. We know that this man is a sinner."

He replied: "Whether He's a sinner, I don't know. But one thing I do know: Though I was blind, now I see."

"What did He do to you?" they asked. "How did He open your eyes?"

"I've already told you," he answered, "but you wouldn't listen. Why do you want to hear it again? Do you too want to become His disciples?"

The Pharisees were furious. They threatened the man and made wicked accusations against him. At last they threw him out.

When Jesus heard what the Pharisees had done to the man whose eyes He had opened, He went out to look for him. When He found him, He said, "Do you believe in the Son of God?"

The man answered, "Tell me who He is, Sir, so that I can believe in Him."

Jesus said to him, "You have seen Him, and it is He who is speaking to you now."

"I believe, Lord," said the man who had been born blind, and he worshipped Him.

The Man Who Couldn't Hear or Speak

On yet another day, a man who couldn't hear or speak was brought to Jesus as He was walking along the shores of the Sea of Galilee. His friends begged Jesus to lay His hands upon him and cure him. Taking him apart from the crowd, Jesus put His fingers into his ears and, spitting, He touched his tongue.

Then, looking up to heaven, Jesus sighed and said to him,

"Be opened!" Immediately the man's ears were opened and his tongue was released so that he could hear and speak. The people were astonished and said, "He has done all things well. He has made the deaf to hear and the mute to speak."

The words and gestures of Our Lord when He performed this miracle were so powerful and memorable that they came to be part of the Church's ancient rite of Baptism.

Jesus Heals the Lepers

As we've seen, Jesus healed a number of illnesses and disorders. But perhaps none of them were as terrible as the disease known as leprosy, now known as Hansen's disease. In biblical times, it was like a living death that numbed and deformed the body.

Today leprosy is not nearly as prevalent as it used to be, and modern medical care can cure the disease. But in the time of Our Lord the case of the leper was almost hopeless. The disease was considered by most people to be incurable.

People were so afraid of contracting the disease that they usually drove lepers away from their homes. They never allowed them to set foot again in any city or town, or to mingle with the people in any way whatever. Lepers were often forced to live outdoors, on the rocky hillsides or in the desert.

Their heads were shaved, and they were forced to wear torn clothing and a veil over their faces. That way, anyone who passed by could see at once that they were lepers. If anyone came too near them, the lepers were commanded by the Law to warn them by crying out, "Unclean, unclean!"

From time to time a leper might be cured. Then, according to the Law of Moses, he had to go and show himself to a priest in the Temple. For eight days he would remain in seclusion, washing his body again and again, according to the ritual of purification prescribed in the Law. At the end of this time the priest would proclaim to the people that the patient had been cured.

One day, Our Lord met ten lepers as He was passing from Galilee to Samaria on His way to Jerusalem. They stood far away, as they were required to do by the Law, but they cried out loudly to Jesus. And instead of saying, "Unclean, unclean!" they shouted, "Jesus, Master, have mercy on us!"

Jesus said to them, "Go, show yourselves to the priest." And as they went their way, obeying Him, they were suddenly cleansed of their leprosy.

One of them, when he saw that he was healed, stopped and turned back. He fell down before Jesus and thanked Him. This man was a Samaritan.

Jesus said, "Weren't ten men healed? Where are the other nine? Was the only man to return and give glory to God this man who isn't even a Jew?"

It was sad enough that nine of the ten men failed to thank Our Lord for the miracle that saved them from such a horrible life. But it was sadder still that the only one who was grateful didn't even belong to the nation that had been called to serve God.

We should often ask ourselves whether we're more like the Samaritan who was healed, or more like the nine others who were healed. God has done so much for us. Do we tell Him often how grateful we are?

CHAPTER 8

Christ Casts Out Demons and Raises the Dead

Jesus Has Authority over Evil Spirits

Those who were healed by Jesus had much to be thankful for. But there were others whose suffering was in some ways an even greater torment than physical illness. Those were the people who were oppressed, and sometimes possessed, by evil spirits. Jesus freed them from their afflictions as well.

Every human being, from Adam and Eve to the present day, has been subject to the temptations and assaults of evil spirits, who are constantly trying to lead us into sin. Even our blessed Savior was tempted by the Devil. But sometimes the evil spirits go much farther than this.

On occasion, demons take possession of a person. The symptom of such possession is that the person has times when he's not in control of himself. The demon takes over his speech and his body movements.

The demon may also torment his victim, inflicting pain, throwing him around, or causing him to suffer some terrible illness. There were many such unfortunate people in Palestine when Our Lord was on earth.

At the beginning of His public life, Jesus was teaching one Sabbath day in the synagogue of Capernaum. He spoke with authority, so the people were listening attentively. Suddenly a voice rang out, "What have You to do with us, Jesus of Nazareth? Have You come to destroy us? I know who You are: the Holy One of God!"

The man who spoke was possessed by a demon. So Jesus rebuked the demon, saying, "Be quiet, and come out of him!" The evil spirit obeyed, crying out and contorting the man's body as it came out. The people were utterly amazed, and soon it was known all over Galilee that Jesus had the power to drive out demons.

The Demon-Possessed Man in the Tombs

The morning after Jesus had calmed the storm on the Sea of Galilee, He and His disciples came to the land of the Gerasenes, which is across the sea from Capernaum. When they stepped off the boat, they saw waiting for them on the shore a tormented man.

He had been possessed by demons for many years. He wore no clothes and lived in a tomb on the hillside outside of town. Night and day he roamed about, screaming horribly and cutting himself with sharp stones. Several times the people had tried to capture him and chain him down, but he would always break even the strongest chains in pieces. No one had the strength to overcome him.

When the possessed man saw Jesus, he fell down on the ground before Him, crying out wildly, "What have I to do with You, Jesus, Son of the Most High God? I beg You by God, don't torment me!"

"What is your name?" Jesus asked him.

The demon answered, "My name is Legion, for we are many."

Legion is a Roman military term for a company of thousands of soldiers. So Jesus knew from this name that the man was possessed, not only by one, but by a great number of demons. They begged Jesus not to drive them away out of the country, but to allow them to enter into a herd of pigs that was feeding on the mountain side.

Jesus gave them permission. The unclean spirits came out of the man and entered the pigs. The whole herd, about two thousand pigs, rushed down the steep hillside into the sea and was drowned.

When the men who were tending the herd saw this, they were terrified and ran away into the city. The news of what had happened spread there and to all the villages nearby. Crowds of people came down to the seashore, and there they found the man out of whom the demons were driven. He was seated at the feet of Jesus, fully clothed and in his right mind.

The Gerasenes didn't want Jesus to remain in their country. They were afraid of His power, and the men who owned the swine resented having lost them. They begged Him to go away, so He climbed aboard the boat and told the apostles to row back to Capernaum.

The man who had been freed from the demons begged to be taken along, but Jesus refused. "Go back home to your friends," He said to him, "and tell them what great things God has done for you." So the man went his way, and he told all through the Decapolis region what Jesus had done for him. And all the people were amazed.

The Demon-Possessed Boy

Once Jesus, Peter, James, and John came down from a mountain to find the other apostles in the valley, surrounded by a great crowd of people. The scribes were arguing with the disciples as the others listened. When the people saw Jesus, they were struck with fear and amazement, and they ran up to Him to speak to Him.

Jesus asked His disciples, "What are you arguing with them about?"

A man pushed through the crowd and said, "Teacher, I brought my son to You, because he has an evil spirit that keeps him from speaking. When the demon seizes him, it throws him to the ground. The boy foams at the mouth and grinds his teeth, and he's wasting away. I spoke to Your disciples and asked them to cast out the evil spirit, but they couldn't do it."

Jesus said, "Bring your son here." While he was coming, the demon began to torment him again. He threw him upon the ground and the boy rolled about, foaming at the lips. "How long has he had this?" Jesus asked the father.

"Since he was a baby," the father answered. "Many times the demon has cast him into the fire and into the water, trying to destroy him. If you can do anything, have compassion on us and help us.'"

Jesus said to him, "If I can? All things are possible to the one who believes."

Bursting into tears, the father of the boy cried out, "I do believe; help my unbelief!"

Then Jesus rebuked the evil spirit and commanded it to come out and never return again. The demon cried out and twisted the boy's body one last time. But at last it left him, and the boy dropped to the ground.

Seeing him lie there motionless, many of the people

said, "He's dead." But Jesus took him by the hand, lifted him up, and gave him back to his father.

That evening the disciples came to Jesus privately and asked Him, "Why couldn't we cast out that demon?"

Jesus said to them, "Because of your lack of faith. For I tell you, if you have faith even the size of a tiny grain of mustard seed, you can say to this mountain, 'Move from here to there,' and it will move. Nothing will be impossible to you."

The Demon-Possessed Girl

The apostles had other opportunities as well for their faith to grow. On one occasion in particular, a woman who wasn't even Jewish proved to them how a great faith in Jesus could help defeat the demons.

In the spring of the third year of His public life, our blessed Savior was teaching in the vicinity of Tyre and Sidon, two Canaanite cities. A woman came to Him and begged: "Have mercy on me, O Lord, Son of David. My daughter is terribly tormented by a demon!"

Jesus wanted to test her faith and her persistence, so at first He said nothing to her. But she followed after Him, still crying out. So His disciples said to Him, "Send her away! She's bothering us."

Finally Jesus said to the woman, "I was sent only to the lost sheep of the house of Israel." By this He meant that His mission was first to the Jews, the chosen people of God. Only later on would His Gospel be preached to the Gentiles.

But the woman knelt before Him and said, "Lord, help me!"

Jesus, still testing her, answered: "It's not good to take the bread of the children and to throw it to the dogs."

"Yes, Lord," she said, "but even the dogs eat the crumbs that fall from the table of their masters."

The woman had persevered and passed the test. So Jesus said, "Woman, your faith is great! It will be done for you as you desire."

Rising up, the woman hurried home. There, she found that her daughter had been healed.

Our Lord performed all these miracles to prove that He is God and can do the things that only God can do. But He also worked them because He loved human beings, and His heart was touched at the sight of their sufferings. Seeing the miracles of our blessed Savior, the people were reminded of the words of Isaiah the prophet:

"Say to those who are faint-hearted, take courage, and don't be afraid! . . . God Himself will come to save you. Then the eyes of the blind will be opened, and the ears of the deaf unstopped. Then will the lame man leap like a deer, and the tongue of the mute will sing for joy!"

Jesus Raises the Widow's Son

As great as Jesus' power was to cast out demons, He had even greater power: He could raise the dead to life! Three times Our Lord showed that He had power over life and death.

One day, as He and His disciples were entering a little town in Galilee called Nain, they met a funeral procession. The body of a young man was being carried out. He had been the only son of his mother, who was a widow. Many people of the city were accompanying the body to the graveside.

Seeing the bereaved widow, Jesus had compassion on her and said to her, "Don't weep." Then turning, He touched the wooden frame on which the body was being carried, and those who carried it stood still. Jesus said, "Young man, I say to you, get up."

At once the dead man sat up and began to speak. Jesus gave him to his mother. Great fear gripped all those who saw what had happened. They glorified God, saying, "A great prophet has arisen among us, and God has visited His people!"

The Daughter of Jairus

The daughter of Jairus, the ruler of the synagogue at Capernaum, was dying. She was only twelve years old, his only daughter. So her heartbroken father came to Jesus, who was teaching in the city at that time. Falling at His feet, he begged Him to come to his house and cure his daughter.

Jesus started at once for the house of Jairus, but the people crowded around Him, and His progress through the streets was slow. Suddenly a messenger came to Jairus, saying to him, "Your daughter is dead. Why trouble the Teacher any further?"

But when He heard this, Jesus said, "Don't be afraid. Only believe, and she'll be well."

When He came to the house, He wouldn't allow anyone to enter with Him except Peter, James, and John, and the parents of the little girl. Inside, many people were standing about, weeping and wailing loudly.

Jesus said to them, "Don't weep. The girl isn't dead, but only sleeping." But they knew that she was dead, and they laughed Him to scorn.

So He sent them all outside and took the child's parents and His three apostles into the room where the girl was lying. Taking her by the hand, He said, "Little girl, I say to you, get up." Immediately she got up and began walking around. Then Jesus told her joyful and astonished parents to give her something to eat.

Jesus' Friend Lazarus Dies

The third person to be raised from the dead was a man named Lazarus, a close friend of Jesus. He lived in the town of Bethany, near Jerusalem, with his sisters, Mary and Martha.

One day Lazarus grew deathly ill, so his sisters sent a message to Jesus, saying, "Lord . . . the one you love is sick." Now, in spite of the great love that Jesus had for Lazarus, and for Mary and Martha, his sisters, He didn't go right away to Bethany. He stayed where He was for two days longer.

His apostles wondered why He delayed so long, but

finally He said to them, "Lazarus, our friend, is asleep, but I'm going to awaken him from his sleep."

The apostles said, "Lord, if he's only sleeping, he'll get well." Now Jesus had actually spoken of his death, but they thought He meant that Lazarus was just asleep.

Then Jesus said to them plainly, "Lazarus is dead. And I'm glad for your sakes that I wasn't there, so that you'll believe. But let's go to him."

They set out for Bethany, and when they arrived, they found that Lazarus had been in his tomb four days. The house was crowded with friends of Mary and Martha, who had come to comfort them in the loss of their brother. Hearing that Jesus was coming, Martha went out to meet Him, but Mary remained in the house.

When Martha saw Jesus, she said, "Lord, if You had been here, my brother wouldn't have died. And even now I know that whatever You ask of God, God will give You."

Jesus said to her, "Your brother will rise again."

Martha replied, "I know that he will rise again in the resurrection at the end of the world."

Jesus said to her, "I am the resurrection and the life. Whoever believes in Me, even if he dies, he will live. And whoever lives and believes in Me will never die. Do you believe this?"

"Yes, Lord," Martha answered. "I believe that You are the Christ, the Son of God, who has come into the world." Then she hurried back to the house and said to Mary quietly, "The Teacher is here and is calling for you."

Lazarus Is Raised From the Dead

Jesus had not yet come into the village, but was still at the place where Martha had met Him. Getting up, Mary ran out to meet Him. When she came to Him, she fell down at His feet and said, "Lord, if you had been here, my brother wouldn't have died."

The heart of Jesus was deeply touched by Mary's grief. Her friends had followed her out of the house, because they thought she had gotten up to go to the tomb to weep there. When Jesus saw Mary and her friends weeping, He was deeply moved.

Jesus asked, "Where have you laid him?"

They replied, "Lord, come and see."

Then Jesus, too, began to weep. Those nearby said, "See how He loved him!" But others said, "If He could open the eyes of the man born blind, couldn't He have kept this man from dying?"

So they came to the tomb. Like many tombs of that day, it was a cave cut out of a rock, and a stone was placed in front of it. Jesus said, "Take away the stone."

Martha said, "But Lord, by this time there will be an odor, for he has been dead four days."

Jesus answered, "Didn't I tell you that if you believe, you'll see the glory of God?" So they took the stone away.

Then Jesus, lifting up His eyes, prayed: "Father, I give You thanks that You've heard Me. I knew that You always hear Me, but I've said this for the sake of the people standing nearby, so that they can believe that You have sent Me."

Then, crying out with a loud voice, He said, "Lazarus, come out!"

Suddenly, Mary and Martha and their friends, and the disciples of Jesus who were gathered around, saw an amazing sight: Lazarus came out of the tomb, still bound hand and foot with bandages, and his face tied up in a cloth. Jesus said, "Unbind him, and let him go." Then He gave Lazarus back to Mary and Martha, his sisters.

The Plot to Kill Jesus

The news that Lazarus had been raised from the dead spread throughout the land. Hearing it, large numbers of the people came to believe that Jesus was the Son of God. Crowds of people from Jerusalem and other places went to Bethany, hoping to see Lazarus. But others went to the Pharisees to tell them what Jesus had done.

The Pharisees went to the chief priests and said, "What will we do? For this man performs many miracles. If we leave Him alone, everyone will believe in Him. Then the Romans will come and take away both our place and our nation." They were worried that the people would declare Jesus their king and revolt against the Romans. But they knew the Romans would easily crush any revolt.

Caiaphas, the high priest that year, stood up and said to them, "You know nothing at all. Nor do you consider how it is expedient for us that one man die for the people, so that the whole nation doesn't perish."

Caiaphas didn't realize it, but by these words he was prophesying that Jesus was the Savior. He wasn't actually speaking for himself; instead, since he was the high priest, the Holy Spirit was speaking through him. In plain words he had prophesied that Jesus would die for the nation. But the Pharisees understood his words as instructions to secure evidence against Jesus that would be strong enough to have Him put to death.

They hoped to find something in His doctrine that sounded like treason against the Law of Moses or against the authority of the Roman emperor. They also sought to have Lazarus put to death, because he was living proof that Jesus was the Messiah, and that the power of God was with Him. But Jesus continued to preach and work miracles, and for the time being, they couldn't stop Him. The hour God had appointed for His ministry to be completed had not yet come.

CHAPTER 9

Christ, the Friend of the Poor

Jesus Lives a Life of Poverty

Our divine Savior knew firsthand the meaning of poverty. He was born in a stable, and His first bed was a manger. Mary and Joseph were poor and had to work hard for a living. His childhood days were spent in a humble little house in Nazareth, a town that was joked about by the people in larger cities.

As a young man, Jesus worked with His hands. He was a carpenter like Joseph, His foster father. His food was the food of the poor; His clothing was that of a working man.

During His public life, Jesus had no home of His own. He and His apostles depended on the charity of the people for their bodily needs. He would send His disciples into a field to gather the wheat that the owners had left behind for the poor.

Our Lord ate when and where He was invited. He slept wherever His friends gave Him a bed. Many nights

He slept outdoors with only the starry skies overhead for a roof.

Blessed Are the Poor in Spirit

Jesus began His wonderful Sermon on the Mount with the words, "Blessed are the poor in spirit, for theirs is the kingdom of heaven." The poor in spirit are those whose hearts are not set on the things of this world. They may be terribly poor and have scarcely enough to survive. But if they bear their circumstances patiently, their reward will be the kingdom of heaven.

Other people are poor because they have willingly given up all that they own for the love of Jesus. They too will possess the kingdom of heaven.

But even those who possess great wealth may be poor in spirit if they use their riches well: not merely for their own comfort and enjoyment, but for the glory of God and the good of their fellow human beings. Theirs, too, will be the kingdom of heaven.

The Rich Young Man

One day, a rich young man came to Jesus. He belonged to a noble family, and his character was beyond reproach. He kept the commandments of God and lived an upright life.

But he wasn't satisfied with himself. His heart was on fire with holy ambitions, and he wanted to make better use of his talents and his wealth. He thought that Jesus could advise him what to do.

Coming to the Savior, he asked, "Teacher, what good work must I do to have eternal life?"

Jesus answered, "If you want to enter into life, keep the commandments."

The young man said to Him, "Which ones?"

Jesus answered, "You shall not kill. You shall not commit adultery. You shall not steal. You shall not bear false witness. Honor your father and your mother. And you shall love your neighbor as yourself."

The young man replied, "Teacher, all these commandments I have kept since I was young. What do I still lack?"

Jesus looked at him and loved him. He was so different

from many others of his age, who were thinking only of pleasure and worldly excess. This boy had in him the making of a great saint.

So Jesus called him to the perfect life. "Only one thing is lacking for you," He said. "Go, sell all that you have and give to the poor, and you'll have treasure in heaven. Then come and follow Me."

When the young man heard these words, he became very sad. Turning around, he went away in silence. He had great possessions, and although he felt a great desire to follow Jesus, he didn't have the courage to give them up.

The Burden of Riches

After he had gone, Jesus said to His disciples, "How hard it is for those who have riches to enter the kingdom of God!"

Hearing these words, the apostles were astonished. Though they were poor themselves, it seems that they had not yet learned to love the freedom that comes from being poor for the sake of the kingdom of God. Perhaps deep down in their hearts, they still envied the rich.

So Jesus repeated what He had said to them: "How hard it is for those who trust in riches to enter the kingdom of heaven! It's easier for a camel to squeeze through the eye of a needle, than for a rich man to enter the kingdom of heaven."

But the apostles were more deeply puzzled than before. They said among themselves, "Who, then, can be saved?"

Jesus replied, "With men it is impossible. But not with God. For all things are possible with God."

Jesus meant this: As long as a rich man depends only upon himself and puts his faith in what he possesses, he may be able to purchase for himself all the finest things of this world, but he won't be able to gain the happiness of heaven. If God gives him the grace, however, he may understand the foolishness of his ways before it's too late. If he becomes generous with what he possesses, God will have mercy on him.

Our Lord knew, however, that people with great riches are often so taken up with their money and the things it will buy, they easily forget that all they are, and all they have, belong to God. They think they can live without Him, and they pay little attention to the inspirations of His grace.

Peter said to Jesus, "We've left behind everything to follow You."

Jesus answered, "Truly, I say to you, everyone who has left behind a house, or brothers, or sisters, or mother, or father, or children, or lands for My sake and for the gospel, will receive in this life a hundred times as much . . . and in the age to come, eternal life."

Those who have given up what is most dear to them in order to follow Jesus may seem poor in the eyes of the world. But they will receive back much, much more than they have given up. As a part of the spiritual riches they gain, they will find in the family of God new brothers and sisters, parents and children.

The Widow's Gift to God

One day, Jesus was sitting near the treasury in the Temple. The treasury was the place where the people came to make their offerings of money. He watched as many rich people came to deposit large sums.

Then there came a widow. She gave two small copper coins, worth about a penny together. Because she had lost her husband, she was extremely poor, and this was all she had left.

Calling His disciples to His side, Jesus said to them, "Truly, I say to you, this poor widow has given more than all the rest. For they gave from their abundance, but she in her need has given all she had, even her last little coin."

The Temple Tax

Each year all the Jews, rich and poor alike, whether they lived in Palestine or in other lands, were required by the Law of Moses to pay a tax. It was known as "the Price of the Soul." It was only a half-shekel, a small amount. But with so many people paying it, it brought in a very large sum of money, which was sent to Jerusalem to be used in the service of the Temple.

In the third year of His public life, our blessed Savior came to Capernaum with His apostles. As they were going through the streets, the tax collectors stopped Peter and asked him, "Doesn't your teacher pay the Temple tax?"

Caught off guard, Peter quickly answered, "Yes." But he returned to Jesus wondering whether that was in fact the case.

Before Peter could even ask the question, Jesus said to him, "What do you think, Simon? From whom do the kings of the earth take tribute and tolls: from their own sons, or from others?

"From others," Peter answered.

"Then," said Jesus, "the sons are exempt."

In this way, Jesus was reminding the apostles that as the Son of God, He was not subject to the Temple tax, for He had no need to pay a "price" for His soul.

"Even so," Jesus continued, "so that we won't give offense to them, go to the sea and cast in a hook. Take the first fish you catch, and open its mouth. When you do, you'll find a shekel. Take that and give it to them to pay for Me and for yourself." A shekel was enough to pay the Temple tax for two persons.

Peter obeyed, and He caught a fish with a shekel in its mouth, just as Jesus had said.

The Foolish Pursuit of Riches

In all these ways, by word and by example, Our Lord showed how blessed poverty can be, and how foolish it is to spend our lives in the pursuit of riches. He told the people to beware of greed, for our happiness doesn't consist in the abundance of things we possess.

To emphasize how quickly life passes away, with the loss of all our possessions, Jesus told His disciples a parable:

"The land of a certain rich man yielded abundant crops. So he thought to himself, 'What will I do? I have no room to store my crops. . . . I'll do this: I'll tear down my barns and build larger ones. There I'll store up all my grain and my goods. Then I'll say to my soul, Soul, you have many good things laid up for many years. Take it easy, eat, drink, and be merry!'

"But God said to him, 'You fool! This very night your soul is demanded of you, and you will die. Then who will own those things that you have hoarded?'

"That's how it is for everyone who lays up treasure for himself and is not rich toward God."

The Great Judgment

Our divine Savior was constantly reminding those who followed Him that it was their duty to love their fellow man and to be charitable. "By this all men will know you are My disciples," He said, "if you have love for one another." Again and again He warned the Pharisees that love of their neighbor and the relief of God's poor would prepare them for heaven—not the mere external observance of the letter of the Law.

In order to reveal to all how important charity is in the eyes of God, Jesus painted a picture of the Great Judgment that will take place at the end of the world.

He told His disciples how the sun and the moon will be darkened, and the stars will fall from heaven. There will be a great roaring of the sea. All the peoples of the earth will mourn, and some will faint with fear, waiting for the final destruction of the world.

Then, Jesus said, all people will see Him, the Son of Man, coming in the clouds of heaven with great power and majesty. "He will send out His angels with a loud trumpet call," said Jesus, "and they will gather together His chosen ones from the four winds, from one end of the heaven to the other . . .

"He will sit on His throne of glory, and all the nations will be gathered together before Him, and He will separate them one from another, as the shepherd separates the sheep from the goats. He will set the sheep at His right hand, but the goats at His left.

"Then the King will say to those at His right hand, 'Come, blessed of My Father, take possession of the kingdom prepared for you from the foundation of the world. For I was hungry and you gave Me food; I was thirsty and you gave Me drink; I was a stranger and you took Me in; naked, and you clothed Me; sick, and you visited Me; I was in prison and you came to Me.'

"Then the righteous ones will answer Him, 'Lord, when did we see You hungry and feed You, or thirsty, and give You drink? And when did we see You a stranger, and take You in, or naked, and clothe You? Or when did we see You sick or in prison, and come to You?'

"And the King will answer them: 'Truly, I say to you, as you did it for one of the least of these, My brothers, you did it for Me.'

"Then He will say to those at His left hand, 'Depart from Me, accursed ones, into the eternal fire prepared for the Devil and his angels. For I was hungry and you gave Me no food; I was thirsty and you gave Me no drink; I was a stranger and you did not take Me in; naked, and you did not clothe Me; sick, and in prison, and you did not visit Me.'

"Then they will say to Him, 'Lord, when did we see You hungry, or thirsty, or a stranger, or naked, or sick, or in prison, and did not minister to You?'

"He will answer them, 'Truly, I say to you, as you did not do it for one of the least of these, My brothers, neither did you do it for Me.' And these will go away into eternal punishment, but the righteous into eternal life."

This stern warning of Our Lord should make us examine carefully our way of life. But if we should be tempted to despair, we need only look at what He did to show His power and mercy to all those sought Him out. His loving concern demonstrated clearly that He's willing and able to help all those who come to Him in faith.

CHAPTER 10

Christ Founds His Church

The Kingdom of God on Earth

As we have seen, in His public ministry on earth Jesus taught about God, healed the sick, cast out demons, fed the hungry, and worked other miracles that demonstrated God's love. These actions led up to His death and resurrection, the most important events in history, which brought salvation and opened the gates of heaven to us. But even after Jesus ascended into heaven, His ministry was not complete.

Our Lord did not intend to leave us alone. His plan was to remain on earth in a new way and to continue the work He had begun. The people would no longer see Him in bodily form, but they would see Him, hear Him, and feel the comfort of His presence in the Church that He was to establish. In the Church's Eucharist especially, Our Lord would be present with His people. Through the Church, the kingdom of God that Jesus founded would extend throughout the earth.

One day Our Lord was standing on the shore of the Sea of Galilee. A great crowd gathered around Him and asked Him to preach to them. Near at hand was moored a boat belonging to Simon Peter. Stepping into it, Jesus told Peter to push off a little way from the shore. Sitting down in the boat, He preached to the people who were gathered on the shore.

After He had finished speaking, He said to Simon Peter, "Launch out into the deep, and lower your nets for a catch."

Peter said to Him, "Master, we worked all night without catching anything. But if You say so, I'll lower the nets."

When this was done, they caught so many fish that their nets began to break. So they had to call some men in another boat to come help them. When the net was finally pulled in, it was so heavy with fish that the boat almost sank.

The fishermen were overcome with wonder at this miracle. Peter, kneeling at the feet of Jesus, said, "Leave me, for I'm a sinful man, Lord."

But Jesus said, "Don't be afraid. From now on, you'll be catching men." They brought their ships to land. Then they left everything behind them and followed Jesus.

Scripture tells us that the apostles are part of the foundation of the Church. When Jesus called them to follow Him, He began the work of laying that firm foundation.

"On This Rock I Will Build My Church"

Toward the end of His public life, Jesus and the apostles were walking one day through the country to the east of the Jordan River. They were near the town of Caesarea Philippi, when Jesus turned to them suddenly and said, "Who do people say that the Son of Man is?" He was speaking, of course, of Himself.

They answered, "Some say you're John the Baptist; others, that you're Elijah; still others, Jeremiah or one of the prophets."

Jesus said to them, "But who do *you* say that I am?"

Simon Peter answered on behalf of all the rest: "You are the Christ, the Son of the living God."

Then Jesus said to him, "Blessed are you, Simon, son of John, because no man has revealed this to you, but rather My Father who is in heaven. And I say to you: You are Peter, the rock, and on this rock I will build My Church. The gates of hell will not prevail against it. And I will give to you the keys to the kingdom of heaven. Whatever you will bind on earth will be bound also in heaven; and whatever you will loose on earth will be loosed also in heaven."

By these words, our blessed Savior revealed to Simon Peter and to the rest of the apostles the great work that they were to do in the world. Peter would receive the keys to the kingdom of heaven. He would be the one to tell men what they must do to please God and to be saved.

Together with the rest of the apostles, Peter would have the authority from Christ to say what was right and what was wrong, what was true and what was false. God would watch over him and protect him from error, and whatever he commanded would be the law for the Church.

Parables About the Church

Our blessed Savior used comparisons to help the apostles and the people understand what His Church would be like and what her mission would be. One day He spoke of the Church as a vineyard, just as the Old Testament prophets had sometimes compared God's people to a vineyard. Jesus said:

"I am the true vine, and My Father is the vinedresser.

Every branch in Me that bears no fruit He will take away; and every branch that bears fruit, He will prune, so that it can bear more fruit.

"Remain in Me, and I in you. Just as the branch cannot bear fruit by itself, but must remain on the vine, so neither can you bear fruit unless you remain in Me. I am the vine; you are the branches. Whoever remains in Me and I in him bears much fruit. For without Me, you can do nothing.

"Anyone who does not remain in Me will be cast out as a branch and will wither. And they will gather him up and cast him into the fire, and he will burn."

The Good Shepherd and the Sheep

Another comparison Jesus made to explain the Church was to say it was like a flock of sheep. This was a useful comparison because raising sheep was one of the principal occupations of the people in the days of Our Lord. No figure was more familiar than that of the shepherd watching over his sheep.

All day long the shepherd would lead his flock across the countryside in search of good pasture. He would watch over them with loving care, driving them gently with his crooked staff. The sheep would learn to know his voice, and when he called, they would come scampering to his feet.

When nighttime came, he would lead them to the sheepfold. This was a kind of yard, surrounded by a stone wall. There was a narrow gate where the sheep would enter while the shepherd stood and counted them as they went in, making sure that none had been lost. Once they were inside, the shepherd would close the gate and bar it for the night.

Then, stretching out on the ground in front of it, the shepherd would go to sleep. But even while asleep he would be alert. If there were even so much as the sound of a stranger's footstep or the rustle of a prowling animal, at once he would be wide awake, ready to protect his sheep.

Sometimes the shepherd didn't own the sheep, but had hired himself out to take care of them for someone else. He was known as a hireling. In that case he might not be very careful about his work. Maybe he would neglect them, or in time of danger he might run away, because the sheep didn't belong to him, and he had little to lose if anything happened to them.

In the Old Testament, King David had spoken of the Lord as his shepherd, tending His flock with love. In a similar way, our Savior compared His Church to a sheepfold and Himself to a shepherd. He said:

"Truly, truly, I say to you: Whoever enters the sheepfold, not by the door but by climbing in another way, is a thief and a robber. But whoever enters in by the door is the shepherd of the sheep.

"To him the gatekeeper opens. The sheep hear his voice, and he calls his own sheep by name and leads them out. And when he has let out his own sheep, He goes in front of them, and the sheep follow him because they know his voice. But they won't follow a stranger. They run from him because they don't know the voice of strangers . . .

"The thief comes only to steal, and kill, and destroy. But I have come so that they may have life, and have it more abundantly.

"I am the good shepherd. The good shepherd gives his life for his sheep. But the hireling is not the shepherd, and the sheep don't belong to him.

"When the hireling sees a wolf coming, he runs away and leaves the sheep unguarded. Then the wolf snatches and scatters the sheep. The hireling runs away because he's a hireling, and he has no concern for the sheep.

"I am the good shepherd. I know mine and mine know Me, just as the Father knows Me and I know the Father; and I lay down My life for My sheep. But I have other sheep as well that are not of this sheepfold. I must bring them as well, and they will listen to My voice, and there will be one fold and one shepherd."

Our Lord was teaching here that His flock of sheep would include not only the Jewish people, but the Gentiles as well. Together, they would make a single flock with one Shepherd, Jesus Himself.

Weeds Among the Wheat

Sometimes Jesus told parables in order to teach about the Church. He told one such story in order to warn His followers that not all the members of His Church would be worthy of the great vocation to which they had been called. Some would fail to be true to His teaching and would lead sinful lives. Our Lord foretold this situation in the following parable:

"The kingdom of heaven," He said, "is like a man who sowed good seed in his field. But while everyone was sleeping, his enemy came and sowed weeds among the wheat, and went away. When the plants came up and bore grain, then the weeds appeared as well.

"The servants of the man's house came to him and said, 'Sir, didn't you sow good seed in your field? Then why does it have weeds?'

"He said to them, 'An enemy has done this.'

"The servants said to him, 'Do you want us to go and pull up the weeds?'

"He replied, 'No. When you pull up the weeds, you may uproot the wheat together with it. Let both grow until the harvest, and at harvest time I'll say to the reapers, Pull up first the weeds and bind them into bundles to burn. But gather the wheat into my barn.' "

His disciples said to Him, "Explain to us the parable of the weeds in the field."

Jesus said, "The One who sows the good seed is the Son of Man. The field is the world, and the good seed are the children of the kingdom, while the weeds are the children of the wicked one. The enemy who sowed them is the Devil.

"The harvest is the end of the world, and the reapers are the angels. Just as the weeds, then, are gathered up and burned in the fire, so it will be at the end of the world. The Son of Man will send His angels, and they will gather out of His kingdom all who cause scandal and those who do evil. Then they will cast them into the furnace of fire, where there will be weeping and grinding of teeth. But the righteous will shine like the sun in the kingdom of their Father."

The Fishing Net and the Mustard Seed

Jesus used other parables as well to teach about His Church. He once said the Church is like a net that's cast into the sea and gathers up all kinds of fish. When the net is full, the fishermen draw it out. Then, sitting by the shore, they pick out the good fish and throw the bad ones away. It will be the same, Our Lord said, at the end of the world, when the angels will separate those who are wicked from those who are righteous.

On another occasion Jesus spoke a parable about the tiny mustard seed. "What is the kingdom of God like," He asked, "and to what will we compare it? It's like a grain of mustard seed that a man took and sowed in his field. It's the smallest of all seeds, but when it grows up it's larger than any herb and becomes a tree, so that the birds of the air come and live in its branches."

How does this parable apply to the Church? When Jesus established it, the Church began as a tiny group of men and women, small like the mustard seed. But in time it grew and grew until its branches stretched out into all the world, and people from every nation have come to make their home there.

More Parables

In order to show the people how important it is to belong to the Church, and how we must be ready to make every sacrifice to possess the kingdom of heaven, the Savior told these two brief parables:

"The kingdom of heaven is like a treasure hidden in a field. A man finds it and hides it again. Then in his joy he goes and sells all he has to buy that field.

"Again, the kingdom of heaven is like a merchant in search of fine pearls. When he finds a single pearl of great price, he goes and sells all he has and buys it."

The mere fact that we belong to the Church doesn't in itself make us fit for the kingdom of heaven. It's necessary to live a holy life. Our Lord compares our good works to the fruit of a tree. A good tree produces good fruit. A bad tree produces bad fruit.

Jesus illustrated this truth for His listeners by the parable of the barren fig tree. He said:

"A certain man had a fig tree planted in his vineyard. He came looking for fruit on it, but he found none. Then he said to the vinedresser, 'Look! For three years I've come seeking fruit on this tree, and I've found none. So cut it down. Why let it use up the ground?'

"The vinedresser said to him, 'Sir, let it alone this year, too, till I dig around it and fertilize it. Perhaps it will bear fruit then. If not, I'll cut it down.'"

This story reminds us that God is merciful, giving us every opportunity to bear fruit. But if we continue to reject His grace, eventually we'll face His judgment. To remain in His kingdom, we must bear good fruit.

Jesus and His Relatives

Jesus made another important point about the nature of the Church one day when a crowd was gathered around Him in a house at Capernaum. Mary, His mother, came to the house to see Him, along with some of His relatives. Someone noticed them standing outside the door and said to Jesus, "Look! Your mother and your relatives stand outside, asking for you."

Jesus said, "Who is My mother, and who are My brothers and sisters?" Then, reaching out His hand toward His disciples, He said, "Here are My mother and My brothers and sisters. For whoever does the will of My Father in heaven is My brother and sister and mother."

By these words our Savior certainly did not intend any disrespect to His blessed mother. He simply wanted the people to understand that all those who do God's holy will aren't just His disciples; they are also members of His family. That family is the Church.

No one ever obeyed the will of the Father in heaven more perfectly than Mary. That's why she was chosen to be, not only the Mother of God, but also the Mother of the Church. In seeking to imitate her perfect model of faith and obedience, we find our place in God's family.

The Parable of the Talents

Yet another parable that Jesus told shows how not everyone called to be members of His Church will receive the same graces. God, in His providence, gives some more, and others less. But whether we have little or much, we must work with what we have. When we do, God will reward our efforts. Jesus said:

"A certain man was about to go on a journey. He called his servants and entrusted his property to them. To one he gave five talents, to another, two, and to another, one—to each according to his particular ability. Then he set out on his journey.

"Now, the one who had received the five talents went and traded with them, and gained five more. In the same way, the one who had received the two talents gained two more. But the one who had received the one talent went away and dug a hole in the earth, where he hid his master's money.

"After a long time, the master of those servants returned and settled accounts with them. The one who had received the five talents came and brought five more, saying, 'Master, you entrusted me with five talents. Look! I've gained five more as well.'

"His master said to him, 'Well done, good and faithful servant. Because you've been faithful over a few things, I'll place you over many. Enter into the joy of your master.'

"The one who had received the two talents also came and said, 'Master, you entrusted me with two talents. Look! I've gained two more as well.'

"His master said to him, 'Well done, good and faithful servant. Because you've been faithful over a few things, I'll place you over many. Enter into the joy of your master.'

"But the one who had received the one talent came and said, 'Master, I know that you are a stern man. You reap even where you haven't sowed, and you gather even where you haven't separated the grain from the chaff. Since I was afraid, I went away and buried your talent in the earth. Look! You now receive back from me what's yours.'

"But his master answered, 'You wicked and lazy servant! So you knew that I reap even where I haven't sowed, and I gather even where I haven't separated the grain from the chaff? If that were true, you should have at least entrusted my money to the bankers! Then when I returned, I would have gotten back what was mine with interest.

" 'Now take the one talent from him and give it to the one who has ten talents. For to everyone who has, more will be given, and he'll have an abundance. But from the one who doesn't have, even what he seems to have will be taken away.' "

By this parable, Jesus was teaching the importance of making good use of God's gifts to us. Whichever particular talents we may have, our responsibility is to cultivate them so that our contribution to God's kingdom, and all the world around us, will be multiplied. On the other hand, if we fail to develop a talent, we could eventually lose it.

Good Soil and Bad Soil

For three years Jesus preached to the people, using parables such as these. Every day, the crowds would gather around Him, and He would speak to them about the kingdom of heaven. They would listen to Him most attentively. They knew that His doctrine was true, and in their hearts they felt a great desire to follow Him. But in the end, very few of them put their desires into practice.

Perhaps the apostles wondered about this strange situation and talked about it among themselves. In order to explain what seemed to them a mystery, Jesus told yet another parable.

"A farmer went out to sow his seed," Jesus said. "And as he sowed, some of the seed fell on the path. It was trampled underfoot by those who walked along, and the birds of the air ate it up.

"Other seed fell on the rock. As soon as it grew up, it withered away, because it had no moisture.

"Still other seed fell among thorns. But the thorns grew up with it and choked it.

"Finally, some seed fell on good ground. It sprang up and yielded grain a hundredfold."

Later on, when they were alone, the disciples asked Jesus the meaning of this parable. He explained it this way:

"The seed is the word of God. Those on the path are those who have heard it. Then the Devil comes and takes the word away from their heart, so that they cannot believe and be saved.

"Those on the rock are those who, when they hear

the word, receive it with joy. But they have no roots. So they believe for a while, and in the time of temptation, they fall away.

"As for those who fell among the thorns, they are the ones who have heard the word, but as they go their way, they are choked with the cares and riches and pleasures of this life. So their grain doesn't ripen.

"But those who fell on good soil are the ones who, with a right and good heart, hear the word of God and hold fast to it. They bear grain through patience."

In this way, Jesus explained to His apostles why some people heard His message and changed their lives, while others didn't. Much of the outcome depends on how well a heart is prepared to change.

The Wise and Foolish Maidens

Jesus also taught that He expects those He has called to His kingdom to make the best possible use of the grace He has given them and to labor diligently in His service. They must be ready at all times to give an account of themselves to Christ, their Judge. Death may come suddenly, He noted, "like a thief in the night."

"If the homeowner had known at what hour of the night the thief was coming," Our Lord said, "he certainly would have kept watch, and would not have allowed his house to be broken into. So you also must be ready, for the Son of Man will come at an hour you don't expect."

In Jesus' time, it was a custom that when a bridegroom had to travel from another town to meet his bride for the wedding, the young women in the bridal party would wait for his arrival, then welcome him and escort him to the festivities. If his arrival was delayed and he ended up coming in the dark, they would carry small oil lamps to light the way.

Jesus taught a parable based on this custom, emphasizing how we must be ready for His return to earth. He will be the Bridegroom coming to meet his Bride, the Church.

"The kingdom of heaven," Jesus said, "is like ten maidens who took their lamps and went out to meet the bridegroom. Five of them were foolish, and five were wise. The five foolish ones, when they took their lamps, took no oil with them. But the wise ones did take oil in their vessels with the lamps. Then, since the bridegroom was delayed, they all went to sleep.

"At midnight the cry went out: 'Look! The bridegroom is coming. Go out to meet him!' So all the maidens got up and prepared their lamps.

"Then the foolish maidens said to the wise ones, 'Give us some of your oil, for our lamps are going out.'

"But the wise maidens answered, 'What if there isn't enough for us and for you? Then all the lamps will go out. You'd better go to the oil merchants and buy some for yourselves.'

"Now, while they were gone to buy the oil, the bridegroom arrived. Those who were ready went with him into the marriage feast, and the door was closed. After a while, the other maidens came and called out, 'Sir, sir, open the door for us!'

"But he replied, 'Truly, I say to you, I don't know you.'"

"So keep watching," Jesus concluded, "because you don't know the day or the hour when I will return."

Jesus Wants to Be Near Us

We don't know for sure when Jesus will return in glory. But until that day, He promised to be with us. The Old Testament book called Proverbs says, "My delights were to be with the children of men." These words express beautifully the great love of the Son of God for the human race.

We want to be near to those we love. So when the Second Person of the Blessed Trinity became Man, His intention was to remain on earth until the end of the world. By showing us how to be good, He could make us happy. By keeping us close to God, He could give us a foretaste of the joys of heaven.

After Our Lord's ascension into heaven, His followers would no longer be able to see Him face to face. But they could see Him in a different way in His Church. As members of the Church, they would be united with Him most closely, as the branches are united with the vine, or as the different parts of the body are joined to the head.

But it wasn't enough for the heart of Jesus to be united with us in a general way. He wanted to unite Himself with each individual soul. To accomplish this, He worked the greatest of all His miracles. He instituted the Blessed Eucharist.

People had to be prepared for this wonder of wonders. He couldn't tell them about it all at once. So He revealed it little by little. But in the beginning, His listeners had trouble understanding and accepting what He taught them about it.

The Bread of Life

Recall the miracle Jesus performed by multiplying the loaves and fishes. That amazing deed was a sign that Jesus cared about people's basic needs, and wanted His disciples to help others. But it was much more than that. This particular miracle gave Our Lord the opportunity to teach about the Eucharist.

After the people had been fed, the apostles got into the boat and started back across the lake for Capernaum.

It was the same night that Jesus came to them, walking on the water.

Now the people knew that Jesus had not gotten into the boat with His apostles. There was another boat near the shore, and they watched all night to see whether Jesus would take it. The next morning they realized that it was useless for them to wait any longer, so they made their way back to Capernaum, looking for Jesus.

There they found Him teaching in the synagogue, and they said to Him, "Rabbi, when did You come here?"

Jesus answered, "Truly, truly, I say to you, you seek Me, not because you've seen miracles, but because you ate your fill of the loaves. Don't labor for the food that perishes, but for the food that endures to eternal life."

"What are we to do," the people asked, "so that we can perform the works of God?"

Jesus answered, "This is the work of God, that you believe in the One whom He has sent."

So they said to Him, "What miraculous sign, then, do you perform, so that we can see it, and believe You? . . . Our forefathers ate the manna in the desert, just as it's written in Scripture, 'He gave them bread from heaven to eat.'" They wanted Jesus to perform a miracle, as God had done when He gave manna to the Israelites for their wilderness journey.

Then Jesus said to them, "Truly, truly, I say to you: Moses didn't give you the bread from heaven, but My Father gives you the true Bread from heaven. For the Bread of God comes down from heaven and gives life to the world."

The people said, "Lord, give us this bread always."

Jesus answered, "I am the Bread of life. Your fathers ate the manna in the desert, and they have died. This is the Bread that comes down from heaven, so that if anyone eats of it, he won't die.

"I am the living Bread that has come down from heaven. Whoever eats this Bread will live forever. And the Bread I will give is My flesh for the life of the world."

Then the people began to murmur among themselves, saying, "How can this man give us His flesh to eat?"

But Jesus continued. "Truly, truly, I say to you: Unless you eat the flesh of the Son of Man and drink His blood, you will not have life in you. Whoever eats My flesh and drinks My blood has eternal life, and I will raise him up on the last day."

Though the people had trouble understanding what

Jesus was teaching, He continued to insist that they would have to eat His flesh and drink His blood to have eternal life. In this way, He laid the groundwork for them to understand later the great gift of the Eucharist, which He would give to the Church. In the Eucharist, Jesus would continue to be with His people, even after He ascended to heaven. And in the Eucharist, He remains with us today.

CHAPTER 11

The Disciples Struggle to Understand

A Kingdom Not of This World

The apostles were with our Savior day in and day out for three years. They traveled with Him on His journeys through the country. They listened to His teaching and saw the miracles He worked.

But they didn't fully understand His teachings. Like many of the Jewish people, they thought that when the Messiah came, He would establish once more the kingdom of their forefathers and conquer all their enemies. When Jesus spoke of the kingdom of heaven, they thought of an earthly kingdom. They knew, for example, what the prophet Isaiah had said about the Messiah:

"For to us a Child is born, to us a Son is given, and the government will be upon His shoulder, and His name will be called 'Wonderful Counselor, Mighty God, Everlasting Father, Prince of Peace. Of the increase of His government and of peace there will be no end, upon the throne of David, and over His kingdom, to establish it, and to uphold it with justice and with righteousness from this time forth and forever."

The disciples took these and other prophecies to mean that they should look for a Messiah who would reign over all the nations of the world as a political ruler. They believed this Messiah would bring the Jews back to Israel from all the places around the world where they had been scattered. There, he would form them into the greatest nation on earth.

This was the great hope of the Jewish people in the time of Our Lord. Jesus knew that they were doomed to disappointment, and He tried to make them understand that the Messiah was not to be an earthly ruler, and that His kingdom was not of this world.

Get Behind Me, Satan!

One day Jesus began to tell His apostles and disciples about the suffering and death He was to undergo. He told them that He would have to go to Jerusalem, where He would suffer many things from His enemies, who would have Him put to death. But after three days He would rise again.

Peter loved Our Lord very dearly. He couldn't bear to hear Him talk about suffering and dying. So He began to argue with Him, saying, "God forbid that this should happen to You!"

Jesus was disappointed in Peter for being so slow to learn. He turned to him and said sternly, "Get behind Me, Satan; you're a hindrance to Me, because you're not concerned about the things of God, but the things of men."

Turning to the other disciples, Jesus said, "If anyone wants to come after Me, let him deny himself, and take up his cross, and follow Me. For whoever wants to save his life will lose it; but whoever loses his life for My sake will find it. What will it profit a man if he gains the whole world, only to forfeit his own soul? Or what will a man give in exchange for his soul?"

Jesus made it clear that being His disciple is not always easy. But following Him is the only way to eternal life. No price is too high to pay for the joy of being with God forever in heaven.

Be the Servant of All

Even the disciples of Jesus sometimes failed to understand how great a price they would have to pay to enter into His kingdom. One day, the mother of James and John, the sons of Zebedee, came to Jesus with her sons. She told Him that she had a favor to ask of Him.

"What do you want?" He asked her.

She answered, "Command that these two sons of mine may sit, one at your right hand and the other at your left, in your kingdom." She was asking for Christ to grant her sons in His kingdom the two greatest positions of honor and authority after Christ Himself.

Jesus turned to James and John and said: "You don't know what you're asking for. Can you drink the cup that I will drink?"

The "cup" Jesus was talking about was the great suffering He would have to endure. He was asking whether the two disciples were prepared to share in His suffering.

James and John answered confidently, "We can."

Then Jesus answered: "You will certainly drink from My cup. But as for sitting at My right or at My left hand, that request is not Mine to grant. These positions belong to those for whom My Father has prepared them."

The other apostles were indignant that James and John

and their mother had made such a request. So Jesus called them all together and said:

"You know that the rulers of the Gentiles lord it over them, and their great men exercise authority over them. But it will not be that way among you. On the contrary, whoever wants to become great among you must be your servant. . . . For the Son of Man has not come to be served, but to serve, and to give His life as a ransom for many."

Jesus's disciples had much to learn about being leaders who serve. And there were other occasions as well when Our Lord had to correct their thinking and attitudes.

Jesus Corrects His Disciples

Once when Jesus was on His way to Jerusalem to celebrate the Feast of Tabernacles, He passed through Samaria. As they neared the town, the Savior sent some of His disciples ahead to find lodging for the night. But the Samaritans refused them hospitality, because they were Jews on their way to Jerusalem.

The disciples came back and told Jesus what had happened. James and John were furious. They said, "Lord, do you want us to call fire down from heaven and burn them up?" No wonder Jesus had nicknamed these two disciples "the Sons of Thunder." Their anger could rumble sometimes like storm clouds!

But Jesus rebuked them. "The Son of Man came not to destroy souls," He said, "but to save them."

Another day, John came to Jesus and said, "Teacher, we saw a man casting out demons in Your name. We told him to stop, because he's not with us."

But Jesus said, "Don't tell him to stop. No one who works a miracle in My name will be able soon after to speak against Me. For whoever is not against us is for us."

Jesus and the Little Children

One day some mothers brought their little children to Jesus so He could lay his hands on them and bless them. Knowing that Jesus had been working very hard and was tired out from His labors, the apostles scolded the mothers for not being more thoughtful. They tried to send the children away.

When Jesus saw this, He was displeased and said to the apostles: "Let the little children come to Me, and don't keep them away, for the kingdom of God belongs to such as these. Truly, I say to you, whoever doesn't receive the kingdom of God like a child won't enter it."

Taking the children into his arms, He embraced them. Then, laying His hands on them, He blessed them.

On yet another occasion our blessed Savior spoke to His disciples about children.

"Whoever receives a little child in My name," He said, "receives Me. But whoever causes one of these little ones who believe in Me to sin, it would be better for him to have a great millstone hung around his neck, and to be drowned in the depths of the sea . . .

"See that you don't despise one of these little ones. For I tell you, their angels in heaven are always beholding the face of My Father in heaven."

A Hard Saying

As we have seen, yet another teaching of Jesus that His followers had a difficult time understanding and believing was His claim to be the Bread of Life from heaven. Hearing this, many people began to murmur again, saying, "Isn't this Jesus, the son of Joseph, whose father and mother we know? How, then, can He say, 'I have come down from heaven'?"

Even His disciples were troubled at the words He spoke. Many of them said, "This saying is hard to accept; who can listen to it?"

Turning to them, Jesus said, "Do you take offense at this? . . . Remember, it is the spirit that gives life; the flesh is of no avail. The words that I have spoken to you are spirit and life. And yet there are some of you who don't believe."

Jesus knew from the beginning that some of His disciples would not believe in Him, and that one of His apostles would actually betray Him. He said, "This is why I told you that no one can come to Me unless My Father grants it." After this, many of His disciples went back to their homes and no longer followed Him.

Turning to the twelve apostles, Jesus said, "Will you also go away?"

Simon Peter answered Him, "Lord, to whom will we go? You have the words of eternal life. And we have believed and have come to know that You are the Christ, the Son of God."

Once again, Peter spoke for the whole group, making a confession of faith in Jesus. But as we'll see, his faith, and the faith of all the others, would one day be tested severely.

The Transfiguration

Try as they might, the apostles could not bring themselves to believe that Jesus was to suffer and die. Their hearts were filled with sadness to hear Him talk about what lay ahead. It was a great disappointment to them to know that all their dreams of an earthly kingdom were in vain.

Jesus knew what they were thinking. He saw the troubled looks on their faces, and He felt a great compassion for them. After all, most of them were just simple, hard-working men, and they had been brought up to believe that the Messiah would be an earthly king. They could not imagine a kingdom that was not of this world. So Jesus decided to show them His glory.

The disciples happened to be with Jesus in the country around Mount Tabor, one of the highest mountains in Palestine. Taking with him Peter, James, and John, Jesus went up to the top of the mountain to pray.

While He was praying, a great change came over Him. His face shone like the sun, and His clothing became white as snow, as bright as lightning. He was entirely *transfigured*—that is, His appearance was transformed.

Suddenly, two men appeared and began to talk with Jesus. One was Moses; the other was the prophet Elijah. The three apostles listened and heard them speaking about His death that would soon take place in Jerusalem.

Seeing that Moses and Elijah were about to leave, Peter cried out to Jesus, "Lord, it's good for us to be here. Let's make three tents: one for you, one for Moses, and one for Elijah."

As Peter was still speaking, a bright cloud came and overshadowed them on the mountain. Out of the cloud, they heard a voice saying, "This is My beloved Son, in whom I am well pleased. Listen to Him!"

Terror filled the hearts of Peter, James, and John, and they fell upon their faces. Then someone touched them, and they heard a voice saying, "Get up. Don't be afraid." Lifting up their eyes, they saw no one but Jesus.

As they started down the mountain with Jesus, He said to them, "Don't tell anyone what you have seen here until the Son of Man has risen from the dead." In this way, He reassured them, both that He would rise from the dead, and that He was the Messiah.

But there was still much that they couldn't yet understand. They eagerly discussed the Transfiguration among themselves, and they puzzled over the glorious scene they had witnessed.

Though Jesus' followers often failed to grasp His message, we must not judge them too harshly. Our Lord Himself told them that only later, after He returned to heaven, would the Holy Spirit enlighten their understanding. And even today, many centuries later, the Spirit continues to lead the Church into all truth, as Jesus promised.

To their credit, despite their confusion about Jesus' mission, the apostles and many others among His disciples remained faithful to Him. Though many were to fall away, and even one of the apostles would betray Him, in the end those who persevered were rewarded richly—not only with understanding, but with eternal life.

PART THREE

How Christ Redeemed the World and Returned to Heaven

CHAPTER 12

The Enemies of Christ

Jesus Rebukes the Pharisees

Jesus had great compassion for the poor. He was patient with His disciples, kind to the tax collectors, and merciful to sinners. But there was one group of people whose attitudes and behavior called for His frequent rebuke. These were the Pharisees.

Jesus warned His disciples not to be like the Pharisees. "They love the place of honor at feasts," He noted, "and the best seats in the synagogue and the respectful greetings in the market place, and being called 'rabbi' by others."

Our Lord told the Pharisees: "Woe to you, scribes and Pharisees, hypocrites! You're like whitewashed tombs, which outwardly appear beautiful, but inside are full of dead men's bones and all uncleanness. In the same way, you, too, outwardly appear righteous to others, but inwardly you are full of hypocrisy and sin."

What was it that moved the gentle Savior to utter such terrible words as these? It was the kind of hypocritical lives that many of the Pharisees lived.

They were careful to perform all the outward actions that the Law of Moses commanded. But in their hearts there was little true love of God. They thought first of themselves and pretended to be good in order to make an impression on others.

If they fasted, they made sure everyone would know about it. They had no pity on sinners. They neglected the poor.

Jesus said this to the people about the Pharisees: "When you give alms, don't sound a trumpet in the synagogues and in the streets to get attention as the hypocrites do, so they will be honored by men. Truly I say to you, that's all the reward they will get.

"Instead, when you give alms, don't let your left hand know what your right hand is doing, so that your alms may be given in secret. And your heavenly Father, who sees what happens in secret, will reward you.

"When you pray, don't pray as the hypocrites do. They love to stand and pray in the synagogues and on the street corners so they can be seen by others. Truly I say to you, that's all the reward they will get. Instead, when you pray, go into your private room and pray to your Father in secret. And your Father, who sees what happens in secret, will repay you.

"When you fast, don't look gloomy like the hypocrites, who disfigure their faces so that people will know they are fasting. Truly I say to you, that's all the reward they will get. But when you fast, anoint your head and wash your face, so that others won't know you're fasting. Then your Father who sees what happens in secret will repay you."

The Pharisee and the Tax Collector

To make His teaching clear to those who listened to Him, our Savior told them this story:

"Two men went up to the Temple to pray. One was a Pharisee, the other a tax collector. The Pharisee stood and began to pray within his heart: 'O God, I thank You that I am not like the rest of men—robbers, dishonest, adulterers—or even like this tax collector. I fast twice a week, and I give You a tenth of all I possess.'

"But the tax collector stood at a distance and wouldn't even lift up his eyes to heaven. He kept striking his breast, saying, 'O God, be merciful to me, a sinner.'"

Then Jesus said, "I tell you, this man went back to his home justified rather than the other. Because everyone who exalts himself will be humbled, and whoever humbles himself will be exalted."

We should ask ourselves whether we sometimes pray as that Pharisee prayed. Do we confess our sins and humble ourselves before God? Or do we pray as if we're doing God a favor when we serve Him?

The Pharisees and the Sabbath

Jesus rebuked the Pharisees as well about their attitude toward the Sabbath day. The Law of Moses commanded the Jews to keep it holy, and the Pharisees were strict about enforcing this law. They taught the people that almost anything a person does on the Sabbath Day, other than worship and rest, is sinful—even the most innocent type of recreation.

Our Savior condemned this false idea of the Pharisees. He told the people that the Sabbath was made for human beings, not human beings for the Sabbath. God wanted them to look upon the Sabbath as a day of rest and refreshment, when they could raise their hearts to God and gather strength for the work of the coming week. He didn't want the Sabbath to be a day of gloom.

The attitude of many people toward the Sabbath is illustrated by one of the miracles Jesus performed.

In Jerusalem there was a pool named Bethsaida. It was a miraculous place. An angel of the Lord came down at certain times into the pool, and the water was stirred up. The first person who went into the pool after the stirring of the water was cured of whatever sickness he might have. Around the pool there were five porches, where sick, blind, lame, and crippled people lay, waiting for the water to be moved.

One Sabbath day, Jesus came to the pool of Bethsaida. There He found a man who had been unable to walk for thirty-eight years. Jesus saw him lying there and knew that he had been waiting a long time. So He said to him, "Do you want to be healed?"

The sick man answered, "Sir, I have no one to put me into the pool when the water is stirred. By the time that I get there, someone else has gotten there before me."

Jesus said to him, "Get up, pick up your bed, and walk." Immediately the man was cured. He picked up his bed and walked away.

Some People Object to the Healing

As he was going along, some of the people saw him. They said, "This is the Sabbath. You're not allowed to carry your bed on the Sabbath!"

The man said to them, "The One who healed me told me, 'Pick up your bed and walk.'"

They asked him, "Who is the man who said to you, 'Pick up your bed and walk'?" But the man didn't know who it was, and Jesus had disappeared in the crowd.

A little later, Jesus saw the man in the Temple. He said to him, "You're cured. Sin no more, so that nothing worse will happen to you."

The man went his way and told some Jewish leaders that it was Jesus who had healed him. When they heard this, they persecuted Jesus because He did such things on the Sabbath.

Jesus said to them, "My Father works until now, and I work." Hearing this, the religious leaders only hated Jesus the more. They looked for an opportunity to have Him put to death, because He not only broke the Sabbath; He also said that God was His Father, revealing that He was equal to God.

This claim they considered blasphemous. And it would have been, if it weren't true. But it was true: Jesus was the divine Son of God.

The Man With the Withered Hand

On another Sabbath, Jesus was teaching in one of the synagogues. Among those who were listening to Him was a man whose right hand was withered. Some of the Pharisees were present, and they were watching Jesus to see whether He would do something that would give them a chance to accuse Him of breaking the law.

They asked Jesus, "Why are you doing on the Sabbath what's contrary to the Law of Moses?" Jesus knew what was in their minds, so He said to the man with the withered hand, "Come and stand here." The man obeyed.

Then Jesus said to the Pharisees, "I ask you, is it lawful

on the Sabbath to do good or to do evil, to save life or to destroy it?" They didn't answer Him, so He asked them another question: "What man among you, if he has a sheep fall into a pit on the Sabbath, will not work by taking hold of it and lifting it out? How much better is a man than a sheep! So it's lawful to do a good deed on the Sabbath."

Turning to the man, Jesus said, "Stretch out your hand." He stretched out his hand, and immediately it was healed.

Filled with rage, the Pharisees rushed out of the synagogue. They sought out influential men who could help them find a way to have Jesus put to death.

The Parable of the Great Banquet

Many of the Pharisees were strongly attached to earthly riches and pleasures, and they lived worldly lives. Jesus often told them that their manner of living would prevent them from entering the kingdom of heaven. But they believed that they had a right to a place in the kingdom because they were the descendants of Abraham. To correct this false idea, Jesus told them this story:

"A certain man held a great banquet and invited many guests. At the time for the banquet to begin, he sent his servant to those invited to come, because everything was ready. But they began all at once to make excuses.

"The first said to him, 'I just bought a farm and I must go out and see it. Please, consider me excused.'

"Another said, "I just bought five yoke of oxen, and I'm on my way to examine them. Please, consider me excused.'

"And yet another said, 'I just got married, and so I can't come.'

"The servant returned and reported these things to his master. Then the master of the house was angry and said to his servant, 'Go out quickly into the streets and lanes of the city, and bring in here the poor, the crippled, the blind, and the lame.'

"After a while, the servant returned and said, 'Sir, your order has been carried out, and still there is room in the banquet hall.'

"Then the master said to the servant, 'Go out into the highways and hedges, and make them come in, so that my house may be filled. For I tell you that none of those who were invited will taste my banquet.'"

In this way Our Lord tried to make the Pharisees understand that no one had a right to the kingdom of heaven simply because he belonged to a certain nation or people. Only those would be allowed to enter who heeded God's invitation to a new life at the Table He would prepare for them.

Jesus and the Moneychangers

Although the religious leaders could be very exact in observing small details of the Law of Moses, they allowed many grave abuses to creep into the religious life of the people. Our Lord said they were people who "strain out the gnat from their drink, but swallow the camel." For example, many people showed a lack of reverence for the Temple of God.

Merchants and moneychangers had set up their booths in the Court of the Gentiles, and there they carried on their business. The merchants sold the doves, pigeons, and other animals that the people offered to the priests for sacrifice. The moneychangers gave the people Jewish money in exchange for Roman money, since only Jewish coins could be used for the money offerings in the Temple.

One day when Jesus went up to Jerusalem to celebrate the Passover, He saw these merchants and moneychangers as He passed through the Court of the Gentiles.

They were surrounded by crowds of people pushing one another about, with much loud talking and confusion. The House of God had been turned into a market place. Worse yet, the merchants and moneychangers were sometimes driven by greed to demand too much money for their services.

Moved by a holy anger, Jesus made a whip of little cords and, pushing His way through the crowd, he drove the merchants and the moneychangers out of the Temple. He overturned their tables and scattered the money on the ground. The sheep and the oxen He also drove out of the Temple, and to those who sold doves, He said, "Take these things out of here! Don't make My Father's house a house of business."

When the religious leaders saw this, they said to Him, "What sign do You show us that proves You have the authority to do these things?"

Jesus answered: "Isn't it written in Scripture, 'My house will be called a house of prayer for all the nations'? But you have made it a den of thieves."

Then, as a sign of His authority, He said to them, "Destroy this Temple, and in three days I will raise it up."

The religious leaders said, "The building of this Temple has taken forty-six years, and you will raise it up in three days?" But the Temple that He spoke about was not the great building of stone; it was the Temple of His body. When He rose from the dead, His disciples remembered this prophecy.

Jesus Speaks in the Synagogue at Nazareth

One day when Jesus was traveling in Galilee, He came to Nazareth, where He had spent His youth. The people of Nazareth had heard rumors of the wonderful things He and His disciples had done since He left His home.

So when He came into the synagogue with them on the Sabbath day, they asked Him to preach to them.

The synagogue was a long hall, and at one end was a kind of sanctuary. There was no altar in the sanctuary, because sacrifices were never offered in the synagogue. Instead, there was a wooden chest covered with a veil, where the sacred books of Scripture were kept.

Near the center was a raised platform where the rabbi stood to preach. The main body of the synagogue was divided into two parts: One was reserved for the men, and the other for the women.

The services always began with the singing of the Psalms. Then came a prayer, followed by the instruction. A passage from the Scripture was read by the rabbi, just as our priests or deacons today read the Gospel during Mass. The rabbi then explained the passage to the people, pointing out to them the lessons it taught for their daily lives. If some stranger or some prominent man were present, the people would often ask him to mount the platform and speak to them.

At the invitation of the people, Jesus rose up to read. The Book of Isaiah the prophet was handed to Him. Books at that time were written on long scrolls of specially prepared sheep or goat skin, called *parchment.* Jesus unrolled the scroll and read the following passage:

"The Spirit of the Lord is upon Me, because He has anointed Me to bring good news to the poor. He has sent Me to proclaim release to the captives, and recovery of sight to the blind; to set at liberty the oppressed, to proclaim the acceptable year of the Lord, and the day of reward."

Everyone in the synagogue was looking intently at Him as He rolled up the scroll and handed it back to the ruler of the synagogue. Then He began to teach. He said, "Today this Scripture has been fulfilled in your hearing."

He went on to show them how these words of Isaiah the prophet had foretold all the things He had come to do.

Everyone was delighted with His words. They said, "Isn't this Joseph's son?" But soon their delight was turned to anger. They expected Jesus to work miracles for them, as He had done in other parts of the country.

Jesus said to them, "You will surely quote to Me the proverb, 'Physician, heal yourself! What we've heard You did in Capernaum, do here as well in your own town.' But truly I say to you, a prophet is not held in honor in his own country.

"There were many widows in Israel at the time of Elijah, when no rain fell for three years and six months, and there was a great famine over all the land. Yet Elijah was not sent to any of them, but only to a pagan widow in Sarephath, in the land of Sidon. And there were many lepers in Israel in the time of Elisha the prophet; yet not even one of them was cleansed, but only Naaman, the pagan Syrian."

When the people heard this, they became furious. How dare He compare them, the children of Abraham, with pagan women and lepers? They rose from their seats, took hold of Jesus, and dragged Him out of the city to a steep cliff. They intended to throw Him over it, but He walked through the crowd without being harmed. So Jesus left Nazareth and went to Capernaum, another city of Galilee.

Jesus' Enemies Accuse Him

Speaking in the Temple one day, Our Lord said to His opponents, "Which of you can convict Me of sin? If I speak the truth, why don't you believe Me? Whoever is of God hears the words of God. The reason why you don't is that you're not of God."

They answered, "Aren't we right in saying that You're a Samaritan and have a demon?"

Jesus replied, "I don't have a demon. But I honor My Father, and you dishonor Me. Yet I don't seek My own glory. . . . Truly, truly, I tell you, whoever keeps My word will never see death."

"Now we know that you have a demon," they insisted. "Abraham is dead, and the prophets are dead; yet You say, 'Whoever keeps My word will never see death.' Are you greater than our father Abraham, who is dead, and the prophets? Who do You claim to be?"

"If I glorify Myself," Jesus answered, "My glory is nothing. It is My Father who glorifies Me—the One you claim to be your God. But you don't even know Him, though I know Him . . . and keep His word. Abraham, your forefather, rejoiced that he was to see My day. He saw it and was glad."

Hearing this, the religious leaders were furious and said to Him, "You aren't yet fifty years old, and you've seen Abraham?"

Jesus replied solemnly, "Truly, truly, I tell you, before Abraham was, I AM."

The enemies of our Savior knew well the meaning of these words. They remembered how Moses, kneeling before the burning bush, had asked God what he should tell the Israelites in Egypt if they asked him who had sent him to deliver them. God had answered Moses, "Tell them I AM sent you."

By using these same words, Jesus was declaring Himself equal to God. So they took up stones to kill Him for blasphemy. But He escaped from them and left the Temple.

Herod and Jesus

Herod was also an enemy of Jesus. He hated Him because he was afraid of Him. He was a superstitious man, and he thought that Jesus might be John the Baptist returned from the dead.

Once when Jesus was in Galilee, some of the Pharisees came to Him and said, "You'd better get out of here. Herod wants to kill you."

But Jesus wasn't so easily frightened. He said, "Go and tell that fox, 'Look! I cast out demons and perform healings today and tomorrow, and on the third day I will finish My course.' Nevertheless, I must go on my way today and tomorrow and the next day, because it cannot be that a prophet should die outside of Jerusalem."

By these words our Savior showed His great contempt for Herod. He let the king know that he had no power to harm Jesus. He also foretold that He would die, not in Galilee, where His ministry was headquartered, but in Jerusalem.

Division Among the Religious Leaders

The agents of the chief priests and Pharisees dogged the footsteps of our blessed Savior, watching for an opportunity to arrest Him. Yet even they were deeply impressed by His teaching and His holy life.

One day the chief priests and Pharisees sent for them and asked, "Why haven't you brought Him to us?"

They answered, "No man has ever spoken like this man!"

The Pharisees accused them: "Are you also led astray? Have any of the authorities or the Pharisees believed in Him? Only this cursed mob, that doesn't know the Law, follow Him."

Then it was that Nicodemus, who was a member of the Sanhedrin, spoke up. Ever since the night he had come to Jesus to ask Him about the kingdom of heaven, he had been a disciple of our blessed Savior, but in secret. Now he said: "Does our law judge a man without first granting him a hearing to find out what he does?"

"Are you a Galilean, too?" they replied, filled with disdain for anyone from Galilee, including Jesus. "Search the Scriptures," they said, "and you'll see that no prophet comes from Galilee."

Jesus knew that His enemies in Jerusalem were plotting against Him this way. But the time for His suffering and death had not yet come. He had work to do before that day came.

For this reason, He remained outside Jerusalem and stayed in the little town of Ephraim, about sixteen miles northeast of the city. From Ephraim He went also to other small towns and was a frequent visitor at the home of His friends in Bethany.

Jesus' Enemies Look for an Opportunity

Our divine Savior spent the last six months of His public life in and around Jerusalem. Ever since the day when His almighty power had raised Lazarus from the tomb, the chief priests and the Pharisees had been watching His every movement. They hoped that He would do or say something for which they could have Him condemned to death.

It's easy to understand why they would hate Our Lord. Again and again He had spoken against many of them in public and said that their piety was only a mask to cover up the sinfulness of their hearts. Because Jesus had criticized them, the people were beginning to see them as they really were and to realize that they were hypocrites. As a consequence, the chief priests and the Pharisees were beginning to lose their influence with the nation, and they were afraid the people would turn against them.

By this time the faith of some of the people, too, had begun to weaken. They had expected the Messiah to be a warlike leader who would free them from the Romans. They couldn't bring themselves to accept a Messiah whose kingdom was not of this world.

For three years they had been waiting for the moment when Jesus would claim the throne of David and declare a war of independence against the foreign foe that held them in bondage. If He hadn't gotten away after He fed the multitude in the desert, the people would have taken Him by force and tried to make Him king.

When Jesus told them in the synagogue at Capernaum that He would give them His flesh to eat and His blood to drink, their hopes were at an end. They understood at last that He did not intend to establish an earthly kingdom. Their disappointment was deep.

Their love for Him had been selfish. They had followed after Him because they thought He would bring them earthly prosperity. Now their love began to turn into hatred.

No sin that could be committed against the Law of Moses was considered as terrible as blasphemy, for blasphemy is a direct insult to God. Whenever Jesus spoke of God as His Father, or said He had come down from heaven, or forgave people their sins, the Pharisees would murmur against Him and say He was blaspheming.

Yet the Pharisees were afraid to have Jesus arrested and brought before the high priest on a charge of blasphemy. They knew that many others still believed in Him. They had seen the many miracles He had performed, and they couldn't believe that He was a sinner. So these faithful followers of Jesus might riot if the religious leaders moved against Him.

Still, Jesus' enemies persisted in seeking an opportunity to silence Him by killing Him. In the end, they crafted a plot to seize Him under the cover of darkness, away from the crowds, by collaborating with one of His own apostles. And though they knew that the Romans wouldn't allow them to kill Him themselves, they could use their influence—and a few veiled threats—to persuade the local Roman authorities to do the evil deed.

CHAPTER 13

The Last Days of Christ's Ministry

Jesus' Anointing at Bethany

Six days before the Feast of the Passover, Jesus and His apostles came to Bethany, to the home of Mary, Martha, and Lazarus. There a supper was prepared for them. Martha served and Lazarus was among those who ate at the table.

As an act of devotion, Mary took an alabaster jar of expensive ointment and anointed Our Lord's head and feet with it. Then she wiped His feet dry with her hair. The house was filled with the fragrance of the ointment.

Seeing this, Judas Iscariot, one of His apostles, grew indignant. He said, "Why wasn't this ointment sold for three hundred denarii and given to the poor?" Judas said this, not because he really loved the poor, but because he loved money. Jesus had given him charge of the offerings that the people gave them to meet their basic needs. But Judas was stealing from those offerings.

Jesus answered, "Why do you trouble her? She has done a beautiful thing for Me. For the poor you have with you always; whenever you want, you can do them good. But you won't have Me with you always.

"In pouring this ointment on My body, she's preparing Me for My burial. Truly, I tell you, wherever this gospel will be preached throughout the whole world, what she has done will be told in memory of her."

Jesus' Triumphant Entry Into Jerusalem

The next day Jesus left Bethany and set out boldly for Jerusalem. Sending two of His apostles ahead to a little town called Bethphage, near the Mount of Olives, He said to them, "Go into the village opposite you. As soon as you enter you will find a donkey tied, and her colt with her. Untie them and bring them to Me.

"If anyone says anything to you, say, 'The Lord needs them,' and he will let them go immediately."

Now all of this took place so that the words of the prophet would be fulfilled. He had said: "Tell the daughter of Zion, behold your king is coming to you, humble, and mounted on a donkey, and on a colt, the foal of a donkey."

The disciples did as Jesus commanded them. The road was crowded with throngs of people on their way to Jerusalem to celebrate the Feast of the Passover. The donkey and colt were brought to Jesus. The apostles threw their garments over them, and Jesus sat on them.

When the crowds on the road saw Jesus coming, they spread their cloaks on the ground before Him and cut down branches from the trees and spread them on the road. With branches of palm trees in their hands, they crowded around Him and cried out, "Hosanna to the Son of David! Blessed is the One who comes in the name of the Lord! Hosanna in the highest!"

The people were following a popular custom of their day for welcoming a king who was approaching their city. When they said, "Hosanna!"—which means "Save us!"—and they called Jesus "Son of David," they were welcoming Him as the Messiah, the royal descendant of King David, who was coming to save the people from their troubles. Many of the people knew that Jesus had raised Lazarus from the dead and worked other miracles. So they now believed that He was the Christ whom God had promised to send.

A number of Pharisees in the crowd were complaining. They said among themselves, "Don't you see that we've accomplished nothing? Look! The whole world is running after Him."

Some of them went up to Jesus and said, "Teacher, rebuke your disciples."

Jesus answered, "I tell you, if these remain silent, the stones will cry out."

Jesus Weeps Over Jerusalem

The procession had now reached the top of the hill, and across the valley they could see the city of Jerusalem gleaming in the sunlight. High over all the houses and other buildings rose the Temple, with its pinnacle pointing toward heaven.

Jesus told them to stop a moment. For a while He gazed on the city silently. Then He began to weep.

"Jerusalem, Jerusalem," He cried out, "you who kill the prophets and stone those who are sent to you! How often would I have gathered together your children as a hen gathers her chicks under her wing. But you refused.

"If only you knew, even today, the things that make for peace. But now they are hidden from your eyes. For the days will come upon you, when your enemies will besiege you, and surround you and hem you in on every side. They will dash you to the ground, you and your children within you; and they won't leave even a single stone on another, because you didn't know the time of your visitation."

Jesus in Jerusalem

Once they entered the city, they were passing through the narrow streets that led to the Temple. The crowds continued to shout, "Hosanna to the Son of David," and to wave their palm branches in the air. Some people ran out of their houses to see what was going on. "Who is this?" they asked.

The crowds answered, "This is Jesus, the prophet from Nazareth, in Galilee."

At last they reached the Temple. The blind and the lame were brought to Jesus, and He healed them. Crowds of children gathered around Him in the Temple, crying, "Hosanna to the Son of David!"

Seeing this, the chief priests and the scribes were furious. They said to Jesus, "Do you hear what these children are saying?"

Jesus replied: "Yes! Have you never read in Scripture, 'Out of the mouths of babies and infants you have perfected praise'?"

A number of Gentiles were in Jerusalem at that time. The Gospel tells us that they had come to worship at the Passover feast, so perhaps they were converts to the Jewish faith. Seeing the great excitement that Jesus caused when He entered the city, some of these Gentiles became curious.

Coming to Philip, they said, "Sir, we want to see Jesus." Philip called Andrew aside to tell him what they had said, and together they went to Jesus.

Jesus said to them, "The hour has come for the Son of Man to be glorified." He was speaking of His soon-approaching passion, death, and resurrection.

These Gentiles were among the countless millions who, until the end of time, would come from every part of the world to pay homage to Jesus and accept Him as their Savior. After His death, the apostles would go out and preach the Gospel to every nation. And all peoples, from every land and tribe, would give glory to Christ the King.

A Voice From Heaven

But Jesus knew the price He would have to pay for this great victory. The Son of God would have to die on the cross in order to enter into His kingdom. So He said, "Truly, truly, I tell you, unless a grain of wheat falls into the earth and dies, it remains alone. But if it dies, it bears much fruit."

Our Lord was comparing His death and resurrection to the planting of wheat. The death of a single seed leads to a new life of many grains, just as His death would lead to new life for the multitudes who would come to believe in Him.

But all those who would follow Him would have to die to themselves so they could receive this new life. "Whoever loves his life will lose it," Jesus said, "and whoever hates his life in this world will keep it for eternal life."

Our Lord knew that His terrible suffering and death were drawing near. Some of His disciples wanted Him to flee from the troubles ahead. But He knew it was His mission to suffer, die, and rise again for the salvation of the world.

"Now My soul is troubled," He declared. "But what shall I say to God? 'Father, save Me from this hour'? No! This is why I came to this hour. Father, glorify Your name!"

Suddenly, a voice came from heaven, saying, "I have glorified it, and I will glorify it again!"

The crowds heard the sound of the voice from heaven, but they didn't know what it meant. Some of them said it had thundered. Others thought an angel had spoken to Jesus.

But He knew that His disciples needed to hear the Father's declaration from heaven, to strengthen their faith and to prepare them for what was coming. "This voice came," He said, "not for My sake, but for yours. Now judgment has come upon the world. Now the prince of this world, the Devil, will be cast out. But I, when I am lifted up from the earth, will draw all things to Myself."

Jesus' Authority Is Questioned

Entering the Temple, Jesus began to preach to the people. Some of the chief priests and leaders of the people came up to Him and said, "By what authority do you do these things, and who has given you this authority?"

Jesus answered, "I also will ask you a question, and if you answer Me, I'll tell you by what authority I do these things. The baptism of John: was it from heaven, or merely from men?" In this way, Jesus was challenging the religious leaders to admit that they refused to recognize any religious authority but their own.

But they said among themselves, "If we say from heaven, He will say to us, 'Why, then, didn't you believe him?' But what if we say from men?" They were afraid of the people, because they all held John to be a true prophet, and they might stone them.

So they answered Jesus, "We don't know."

Jesus replied, "Neither then will I tell you by what authority I do these things."

Having tried in vain to prove Our Lord guilty of some sin against the Law of Moses, the enemies of our blessed Savior now adopted another course. If they could lead Him to say something against the Roman government, they would be able to go before the Roman governor and accuse Him of treason.

God and Caesar

After the Pharisees had plotted their strategy, they consulted with some of the members of King Herod's court. Then they sent spies to Jesus to try to trap Him in what He said. They pretended that they were sincere Jews who were worried because they didn't know whether it was sinful to pay tribute to the Roman emperor, Caesar.

They said to Jesus, "Teacher, we know that you are

truthful. You teach the way of God in truth, whatever people may say—even people of high status. So tell us what you think: Is it lawful to give tribute to Caesar, or not?"

But Jesus knew what was in their minds, and He wasn't deceived. He said, "Why are you putting me to the test, you hypocrites? Show Me the coin for the tribute."

So they offered Him a denarius, a Roman coin. Jesus asked, "Whose image and inscription are these?"

"Caesar's," they replied.

"So give to Caesar the things that are Caesar's," Jesus said to them. "But give to God the things that are God's."

Amazed at this answer, they left Him and went their way.

Next it was Jesus' turn to pose a tricky question. That same day He said to some Pharisees who were gathered around Him, "What do you think of the Christ? Whose descendant is he?"

They replied to Him, "The descendant of David."

So he quoted one of David's psalms to them. "How is it, then," He asked, "that David, inspired by the Holy Spirit, calls him Lord, saying, 'The Lord said to my Lord: Sit at my right hand, until I make your enemies your footstool'? If David calls the Christ his Lord, how can he be speaking to someone who is his human descendant?"

No one was able to answer Him. The mystery could be understood only in the knowledge that the Christ was both divine and human, as Jesus was. But the Pharisees refused even to consider that possibility. From that day onward, however, no one dared to question Him that way again. Their attempts had failed to trap Him in what he said.

Throughout each day He was teaching in the Temple. But in the evening, after leaving the city, He spent the night on the Mount of Olives.

Judas Agrees to Betray Jesus

The next day the chief priests and the leaders of the people were gathered in the court of the high priest, Caiaphas. They were consulting together about Jesus, trying to think of some way they could arrest Him and put Him to death. The Feast of the Passover was at hand, so Jerusalem was crowded with people, many of whom might rise up and defend Jesus if anyone laid hands on Him. So the chief priest insisted that they must not try to arrest Him during the festival, because the people might riot.

It was then that Satan entered into the heart of Judas Iscariot, one of the twelve apostles. Judas had been with our blessed Savior from the beginning and was the only one of the apostles who came from Judea. He probably knew the ways of the world better than the others, most of whom were poor fishermen, and Jesus seems to have depended on him to look out for the practical side of His mission. He had charge of the money, so he no doubt did most of the buying that was necessary.

Apparently, Judas loved the things of this world. He couldn't get used to the poverty in which our Savior and His apostles lived. He was happy when he had money in his possession, and He probably dreamed of the things that money could buy. In spite of all that Our Lord said, Judas continued to look forward to the day when Jesus would establish a political kingdom here on earth.

Recall that day in Capernaum, when Jesus told the people that He had come, not to give them bread for their bodies, but food for their souls. Perhaps that was the day Judas began to turn against our blessed Lord. He could have left Jesus at any time and gone back to his home. But instead he chose to betray Him.

One day Judas slipped away from the other apostles and went to the chief priests and said to them, "What will you give me if I hand Him over to you?" They offered him thirty pieces of silver. Judas agreed to their price. From that time on, he kept watching for a time when Jesus would be alone and away from the people, so that he could betray Him to His enemies.

CHAPTER 14

Christ at the Last Supper and in the Garden

Preparations for the Passover

It was Thursday, and the Feast of the Passover was at hand. For seven days the Jews would celebrate the anniversary of their deliverance from the hands of the Egyptians. On the first day, according to the ancient ceremony, they would eat the Paschal lamb.

Early in the morning, Jesus sent Peter and John into the city to prepare the Paschal supper for Himself and His disciples. When they asked Him where they should prepare the meal, He answered:

"Go into the city, and there you'll meet a man carrying a pitcher of water. Follow him. In whichever house he enters, say to the head of the household, 'The Teacher says, Where is My guest room, where I am to eat the Passover with My disciples?' He will show you a large, furnished upper room. Prepare for us there."

Peter and John went their way and came into the city. Everything turned out just as Jesus had foretold. They killed a Paschal lamb and roasted it as the Law of Moses commanded.

Once everything was ready, they waited for Jesus and the other apostles to come. When evening arrived, they came and gathered around to eat, with Jesus at the head of the table, and John beside Him.

When they were all in their places, Jesus said, "I have earnestly desired to eat this Passover with you before I suffer."

Jesus Washes His Disciples' Feet

That evening an argument started among the apostles about which of them would be the greatest. But Jesus rebuked them, saying, "Let the greatest among you act as the youngest, and the leader as the one who serves. For who is greater, the one seated at the table, or the one who is serving? Isn't it the one seated at the table? But I am among you as one who serves."

Then Jesus gave to His apostles and to all the world a beautiful lesson of love and humility. Having loved His own who were in this world, He loved them to the end. Getting up, He laid aside His clothes and wrapped a towel around His waist. Then, putting water in a basin, He knelt down and began to wash the feet of His disciples, and to wipe them with the towel.

He knelt first at Peter's feet. Peter said, "Lord, do You intend to wash my feet?"

Jesus said, "What I'm doing now, you don't understand. But you'll understand later."

Peter said to Him, "You'll never wash my feet!"

Jesus answered, "If I don't wash you, you'll have no part in Me."

Hearing this, Peter said, "Lord, not just my feet, but also my hands and my head!"

But Jesus said, "Whoever has bathed needs only to wash his feet, and he is clean all over. And you are clean—but not all of you." For Jesus knew who it was that would betray Him.

After He had washed the feet of all His apostles, Jesus put on His clothes once more and returned to the table.

"Do you know what I have done for you?" He asked them. "You call Me Teacher and Lord, and you're right, for I am. So if I, being your Lord and Teacher, have washed your feet, you also ought to wash one another's feet. For I have given you an example, that you should do as I have done for you. Truly, truly I tell you, the servant is not greater than his master; nor is the one who is sent greater than the one who sent him."

The Betrayer Is Revealed

They now began to eat the Paschal lamb, as the Law commanded. Jesus, acting as the head of the household, would have had the role of explaining the ceremonies as they went along. But while they were eating, Jesus became troubled in spirit, and a great sadness came over Him.

"Truly, truly, I tell you," He said, "one of you will betray Me."

Hearing this, the apostles were shocked and grieved. They began to say to Him one by one, "Am I the one, Lord?"

He answered, "The hand of the one who betrays Me is with Me on the table. For the Son of Man goes His way, as it's written of Him in Scripture. But woe to the man by whom the Son of Man will be betrayed. It would be better for him if he had never been born."

All this time, Judas had remained silent. Now he leaned forward and said, "Am I the one, Rabbi?"

Jesus answered him in a low voice, "You have said so."

John, the disciple whom Jesus loved, leaned over and rested his head on Our Lord's chest. Peter made a sign to him to ask Jesus which apostle He was talking about. John whispered, "Lord, who is it?"

In a low voice, Jesus answered, "The one to whom I will give this morsel when I have dipped it."

Now there was a dish on the table filled with a mixture of fruits: apples and figs and citron. The cinnamon and other spices used in its preparation gave it a reddish color, and it reminded the Jews of the bricks their forefathers had to make before God delivered them from Egypt. Into this dish Jesus dipped a morsel of bread and handed it to Judas, saying to him, "What you plan to do, do quickly."

Only John understood what Jesus meant. The other apostles thought Jesus meant that Judas should buy the things they would need for the festival day, or that he should give something to the poor. When Judas had received the bread from the hands of our blessed Savior, he went out immediately, and it was night.

Jesus Institutes the Holy Eucharist

Then Jesus took in His hand a piece of the unleavened bread that was part of the Paschal meal. Giving thanks to God, He blessed it, broke it, and gave it to His apostles, saying, "Take and eat; this is My body."

Then He took a large chalice filled with wine and gave thanks. He passed it to them, saying, "All of you drink of this, for this is My blood of the new covenant, which will be shed for many for the forgiveness of sins. But I tell you, I will not drink again of this fruit of the vine until I drink it new with you in the kingdom of My Father."

Now was fulfilled the promise that Jesus had made in the synagogue at Capernaum. He had given His apostles

His flesh to eat and His blood to drink. Then He said, "Do this in remembrance of Me." By these words He gave to them and to their successors, the priests of the Catholic Church, the power to change bread and wine into His Body and Blood, and to offer up until the end of time the Holy Sacrifice of the Mass.

Now would be fulfilled the prophecy of Malachi: "From the rising of the sun even to the setting, My name is great among the Gentiles. And in every place there is a sacrifice, and there is offered to My name a clean offering. For My name is great among the Gentiles, says the Lord of hosts."

With love in their hearts, the apostles received the Body and Blood of their Lord. Then Jesus began to talk with them further.

"Little children," He said, "yet a little while I'll be with you. You'll seek Me when I'm gone. But where I'm going, you can't come. . . . A new commandment I give you, that you love one another. As I have loved you, you should also love one another. By this everyone will know that you're My disciples, if you have love one for another."

Words of Comfort

Seeing how sorrowful they all were, Jesus began to speak words of comfort to them. "Don't let your hearts be troubled," He said. "You believe in God; believe also in Me. In My Father's house there are many rooms; if it weren't so, I would have told you, because I go to prepare a place for you. And if I go to prepare a place for you, I will come again, and will take you to Myself, so that where I am, you also may be."

Thomas said to Him, "Lord, we don't know where you're going; so how can we know the way?"

Jesus said to him, "I am the way, and the truth, and the life. No one comes to the Father, but through Me."

Philip said, "Lord, show us the Father, and that will be enough for us."

Jesus replied, "Have I been with you so long, and you haven't known Me? Philip, the one who sees Me sees the Father also. Don't you believe that I am in the Father, and the Father in Me? The words that I speak to you, I don't speak on My own authority. But the Father dwelling in Me, it's He who does the works . . .

"If you love Me, keep My commandments. And I'll ask the Father, and He'll give you another Advocate to remain with you forever: the Spirit of truth, whom the world cannot receive, because it neither sees Him nor knows Him. But you will know Him, because He'll remain with you, and will be in you. I won't leave you as orphans; I'll come to you . . .

"These things I've spoken to you while I'm still with

you. But the Father will send the Advocate, the Holy Spirit, in My name, and He'll teach you all things, and bring to your mind all that I've said to you.

"Peace I leave with you; My peace I give to you; not as the world gives peace, I give to you. Don't let your hearts be troubled or afraid."

After they had stood up from the table and had sung a hymn, they left the upper room and went out of the city. They walked along the road that led through the Kidron Valley. Crossing the bridge that spanned the Kidron Brook, they climbed the Mount of Olives.

Jesus Predicts Peter's Denial

Then Jesus said to the apostles: "This night you'll all fall away because of Me, for it's written in Scripture, 'I will strike the shepherd, and the sheep of the flock will be scattered.' But after I've risen, I'll go before you into Galilee."

Turning to Simon Peter, Jesus said, "Simon, Simon . . . Satan has desired to have you, so that he can sift you like wheat. But I've prayed for you, that your faith won't fail. And once you've turned again, strengthen your brothers."

Peter said to Him, "Lord, where are You going?"

Jesus answered, "Where I'm going, you can't follow Me right now. But later you'll follow."

Peter said, "Why can't I follow You now? I'll lay down my life for You. I'm ready to go with you both to prison and to death. Even if everyone else falls away from you, I'll never fall away."

Jesus replied, "Will you lay down your life for Me? Truly, truly, I tell you, the rooster won't crow until you've denied Me three times."

But Peter was sure that this could never be. He said, "Even if I should have to die together with you, I won't deny you." And all the other apostles said the same thing.

The Vine and the Branches

As they went along, Jesus continued to teach them. "As the Father has loved Me," He said, "so I have loved you; remain in My love. If you keep My commandments, you will remain in My love . . .

"And this is My commandment, that you love one another as I have loved you. Greater love has no man than this, that he lay down his life for his friends. You are my friends if you do the things that I command you.

"You have not chosen Me. I have chosen you, and appointed you, to go and bear fruit, so that your fruit will remain, and so that whatever you ask the Father in My name, He will give it to you."

Now Jesus paused and, raising His eyes to heaven, He prayed: "Father, the hour has come. Glorify Your Son, so that Your Son can glorify You. You have given Him power over all humankind, so He can give eternal life to all those You have given Him.

"And this is eternal life: that they may know You, the only true God, and Jesus Christ, whom You have sent. I have glorified You on earth; I have finished the work You gave Me to do. Now glorify Me, Father, with Yourself, with the glory I had with You before the world existed."

Jesus Prays in Gethsemane

They had now come to the Garden of Gethsemane, near the foot of the Mount of Olives. Jesus had spent many nights in this little garden. It was in the middle of a grove of olive trees.

The word *Gethsemane* means "olive press." At one time there had been an olive press here, where the olives were crushed to obtain their valuable oil. The place was quiet and secluded, and Jesus loved to go there and spend the night in prayer.

At the gate, Jesus invited Peter, James, and John to come with Him farther into the garden, but told the other eight to sit down and wait for them. As they walked forward, Jesus became deeply troubled. He said to the three apostles, "My soul is sad—sad enough to die. Wait here, and stay awake with Me. Pray so that you won't fall into temptation."

Then He went on alone, about a stone's throw. Falling flat on the ground, He prayed, "Father, if it is possible, let this chalice pass away from Me. Nevertheless, not as I will, but as You will."

Then an angel from heaven appeared to Him, to strengthen Him. Being in agony, He prayed even more earnestly. And His sweat became like drops of blood, trickling down on the ground.

After a long time, He got up and went back to His apostles. He found them sound asleep. Waking Peter, He said, "Peter, couldn't you stay awake one hour with Me? Be alert, and pray that you don't fall into temptation. The spirit indeed is willing, but the flesh is weak."

Going away again, He prayed: "My Father, if this chalice cannot pass away unless I drink it, Your will be done."

Coming back once more to His apostles, again He found them sleeping, for their eyes were heavy. Leaving them, He went again and prayed the third time, saying the same words again.

A third time He returned to His apostles, but this time He said, "Sleep on now, and get your rest. The hour is at hand when the Son of Man will be betrayed into the hands of sinners."

Then He added at last, "Get up, and let's go. Look! The one who betrays Me is at hand."

Jesus Is Arrested

While He was still speaking, they heard a noise in the distance. Voices were calling to one another, and through the trees they could see the glow of torches. It was Judas Iscariot, coming at the head of a band of soldiers and servants sent by the chief priests and the Pharisees. Judas knew he could find Jesus here, because He often came to the Garden of Gethsemane with His apostles.

Armed with swords and clubs, and with lanterns and torches to light their way, the soldiers and servants began to search the garden to find Jesus. Judas had given them a sign, saying, "The one I kiss is the One you want. Seize Him."

Jesus made no attempt to hide from the mob. Instead, He went to meet them. "For whom are you searching?" He asked.

They answered, "Jesus of Nazareth."

Jesus said to them, "I am He."

As soon as Jesus had said "I am He," the mob that was with Judas pulled back and fell to the ground. Then Judas came forward and said, "Hello, Rabbi," and kissed Him.

Jesus said to him, "Judas, are you betraying the Son of Man with a kiss?"

Again Jesus asked them, "For whom are you searching?"

They replied again, "Jesus of Nazareth."

Jesus answered, "I already told you that I am He." Then, pointing to His apostles, He said, "If I'm the One you're looking for, then let these men go their way."

This time the soldiers came up, seized Jesus, and held Him.

When the apostles saw their beloved Master in the hands of these thugs, they cried out, "Lord, should we fight with the sword?" Simon Peter, drawing his sword, struck the servant of the high priest and cut off his right ear. The name of the servant was Malchus.

But Jesus said to Peter, "Put your sword back into its place. All those who take the sword will perish by the sword. Don't you realize that I could ask My Father, and even now He would send ten legions of angels to defend Me? But if I did that, how could the Scriptures be fulfilled that say this must happen? Shouldn't I drink the chalice that the Father has given Me?"

Then Jesus touched the ear of Malchus and healed him. Turning to the crowd, He said, "You've come out here to arrest Me with swords and clubs, as if I were a robber. Yet I sat daily with you, teaching in the Temple, and you never laid hands on Me. But this is your hour, and the power of darkness." Then all His apostles ran away and left Him.

CHAPTER 15

Christ Before His Accusers

Jesus Is Questioned by Annas

Now began the journey back from Gethsemane into Jerusalem. Jesus and His captors crossed the Kidron Brook and soon reached the gates of the city. The soldiers hurried our Savior through the streets and brought Him to the palace of Annas, who was the father-in-law of Caiaphas, the high priest that year.

Formerly, Annas had been high priest himself, but he was deposed by the Roman governor. However, he was still held in great honor by the chief priests and the Pharisees. They believed that the Roman governor, in deposing him, had gone beyond his authority and had unlawfully interfered with their religion, which was no concern of his.

Externally, the religious leaders submitted to the governor's orders. But they continued to view Annas as the real high priest and to follow whatever advice and counsel he might give them. It was through his influence that

Caiaphas, his son-in-law, had been raised to the office of high priest.

Word was now sent out to the members of the Sanhedrin. They were informed that Jesus had been captured, and they were ordered to assemble at once in the house of Caiaphas, to sit in judgment on Him. While they were waiting, Annas began to question Jesus about His teaching and His disciples.

Jesus said to him, "I have spoken openly to the world. I have always taught in the synagogue and in the Temple, where all the Jews come together; and I've said nothing in secret. Why are you asking Me this? Ask all those who have heard what I've taught them. They know what I've said."

One of the servants standing nearby struck Jesus with his hand, saying, "Is that how You answer the high priest?"

Jesus replied, "If I've spoken wrongly, tell us what's wrong; but if I've spoken correctly, why do you strike Me?" Then Annas ordered Jesus to be bound and taken to Caiaphas.

Peter Denies Jesus

The apostles who had told Jesus that they were ready to suffer prison and death with Him had run away at the first sign of danger in the garden. It's true that Peter did pull out his sword and come to our Savior's defense, but when Jesus told him to put away his sword, he too escaped into the darkness of the night. The Shepherd had been struck, and the sheep were scattered.

Peter and John seem to have been the first of the apostles to realize what cowards they had been. Even they were not brave enough to take their place openly at the side of the Savior. They followed Jesus when He was taken back to Jerusalem, but they followed Him at a distance.

John seems to have been known at the palace of the high priest, and he summoned up enough courage to enter with the crowd. But Peter remained outside in the darkness. Before long, John missed him and went back outside to find him. Then John convinced the maid who kept the door to let Peter enter.

Inside the gate was a courtyard, with a fire blazing in the middle. Around it the servants sat warming themselves, for the night was cold. Coming close to the fire, Peter too warmed himself.

A little later, the maid who had allowed Peter inside came to the fire. Seeing him, she looked at him closely and said, "Aren't you too a disciple of Jesus of Nazareth?"

But Peter replied, "Woman, I don't know Him."

After a little while, another maid, seeing him, said, "This man too was with Jesus of Nazareth." Again, Peter denied it with an oath. He said, "I don't know the man."

From where Peter was standing, he could look into the room in the palace where the trial of Jesus was being held. He could see our Savior standing among His accusers.

An hour passed, and Peter began to breathe easier. He felt sure he had convinced those who were standing around the fire that he was not a disciple of Jesus. He began to talk to the man standing next to him.

Looking at him in surprise, the man said, "Certainly you're one of His disciples, because your Galilean accent betrays you."

Hearing this, another of the servants of the high priest came up and looked intently at Peter. Finally he said to him, "Didn't I see you in the garden with Him?" This servant happened to be a relative of Malchus, whose ear Peter had cut off.

Then Peter began to curse and to swear, saying, "I don't know this man you're talking about."

Just then the rooster crowed. Jesus turned and looked at Peter.

Immediately Peter remembered what Jesus had said: "Before the rooster crows, you'll deny Me three times." Bursting into tears, he pushed his way through the crowd, rushed through the gate of the palace, and went outside, weeping bitterly.

Jesus' Trial Before the Sanhedrin

Assembled in the palace where Caiaphas lived, the Sanhedrin were proceeding with the trial of Jesus. From one witness after another they tried to obtain evidence that Jesus had said or done something for which they might condemn Him to death. But their efforts were in vain.

Many came who bore false witness against Jesus. But they contradicted themselves, with no two of them agreeing in their accusations. Finally, they found two witnesses who said, "We heard Him say, 'I am able to destroy the Temple of God, and after three days to rebuild it.'"

At last, the high priest stood up and said to Jesus, "Do you have no reply to what these witnesses say against you?" But Jesus kept silent.

Then the high priest said to Him, "I adjure you by the living God, tell us if you are the Christ, the Son of God."

Jesus answered, "You yourself have said so. And you will see the Son of Man sitting at the right hand of the power of God, and coming in the clouds of heaven."

Acting deeply shocked at these words of our blessed Savior, Caiaphas tore his robe and said, "He has blasphemed. What further need do we have of witnesses? You have heard the blasphemy yourselves; what do you think?"

They all cried out, "He deserves death!"

Now the Sanhedrin could declare someone to be guilty of a crime punishable by death under Jewish law. But they had no power to order his execution. That right belonged solely to the Roman governor, who at that time was Pontius Pilate. So they stood up, ordered Jesus to be bound, and led Him to Pilate.

Judas Hangs Himself

When Judas heard that Our Lord had been condemned to death, he regretted his betrayal. Taking the thirty pieces of silver, he brought them back to the chief priests and elders, saying, "I've sinned in betraying innocent blood."

They replied, "What's that to us? See to it yourself."

Judas threw down the pieces of silver in the Temple. Then he rushed out, ran away, and hung himself.

Gathering up the pieces of silver, the chief priests said, "It's not lawful to put them into the Temple treasury, because it's blood money." After discussing the matter among themselves, they finally decided to use the money to buy a potter's field, the burying place for strangers.

In this way was fulfilled the prophecy of Jeremiah: "And they took the thirty pieces of silver, the price of Him upon whom a price had been set . . . and they gave them for the potter's field."

Jesus on Trial Before Pilate

Meanwhile, Jesus had been brought to the *praetorium,* the palace of the Roman governor, which was in the Antonia. The members of the Sanhedrin remained outside in the Gabbatha because, according to their law, if they entered the house of a Gentile, they would become defiled and would not be allowed to take part in the celebration of the Passover. They were not alone in the large square, for by this time the news of the arrest of Jesus had spread throughout the city, and a great crowd, moved by curiosity or eager for excitement, had flocked to the praetorium.

Jesus was turned over to the Roman guards and sent alone into the palace to face Pontius Pilate. Going outside, he stood on the balcony of the palace and said to the members of the Sanhedrin, "What accusation do you bring against this man?"

They answered, "If He weren't a criminal, we wouldn't have handed Him over to you."

Pilate said, "Take Him yourselves and judge Him according to your own law."

But the Jewish leaders answered, "We're not allowed to put anyone to death."

Pilate wanted to avoid trouble if it at all possible. The city was crowded with visitors, and it was his duty to preserve order. He didn't want a riot to take place. So he decided to question Jesus himself, hoping to learn something he could use as an argument against the Sanhedrin, leading them to change their judgment.

Pilate turned and entered the palace again. Going into the large room where he usually held court, he ordered Jesus to be brought before him. When this was done, he said to our Savior, "Are You the king of the Jews?" If Jesus was publicly claiming to be a Jewish king apart from Roman approval, He could be accused of treason against Rome.

Jesus answered, "Do you say this on your own, or have others said it to you about Me?"

Pilate answered, "Am I a Jew? Your own nation and chief priests have handed You over to me. What have You done?"

Jesus answered, "My kingdom is not of this world. If My kingdom were of this world, My servants would fight to keep Me from being handed over to the Jews."

So Pilate replied, "So You are a king?"

Jesus answered, "You say that I'm a king. This is why I was born, and why I came into the world, to bear witness to the truth. Everyone who is of the truth hears My voice."

Pilate said to Him, "What is truth?" Then, standing up, he left the room and went out once more to the crowd.

Standing on the balcony overlooking the square, Pilate said to the chief priests and the crowds, "I find no guilt in Him."

But they were insistent. Someone shouted, "He's stirring up the people, teaching throughout all Judea, from Galilee to this place."

Herod Questions Jesus

When Pilate heard them mention Galilee, he asked whether Jesus were from Galilee. When he heard that He was, he thought of a plan that would allow the whole affair to be settled without any involvement on his part. Herod Antipas, who had put John the Baptist to death, was visiting Jerusalem, and he was the ruler of Galilee. So Pilate sent Jesus to Herod.

When Herod saw Jesus, he was glad. He had heard the story of the wonderful things Jesus had done in Galilee. Ever since the death of John the Baptist, Herod had been most anxious to see Him, so he could assure himself that Jesus wasn't John the Baptist risen from the dead. Then, too, his curiosity was aroused, and he hoped to see Jesus work a miracle.

Herod asked Jesus one question after another. But our Savior remained silent. All the while, the chief priests and the scribes stood by, repeating their accusations.

The silence of our Savior hurt Herod's vanity. So he began to make fun of Him and mock Him. He ordered his soldiers to put on Him a bright garment, as a sign that He was a fool. Then he sent Him back to Pilate. That same day, Herod and Pilate, who had been enemies, became friends.

The Mob Calls for Barabbas

Once more, Pilate came out and spoke to the people. He said to them, "You've brought this man before me as someone who misleads the people. Look! I've examined Him in your presence and found no guilt in Him with regard to the charges you bring against Him.

"Nor does Herod, for he sent him back to us. Look! He's done nothing worthy of death. So I'll have Him scourged and then release Him." Hearing this, the crowd was furious. They shouted their demand that Pilate put Jesus to death.

Pilate was sitting in the place of judgment, waiting for Jesus to be brought back to him, when his wife sent a message to him. It said: "Have nothing to do with that righteous man; for I have suffered many things this day in a dream because of Him." But the governor could hear the shouts of the mob, and he feared what might happen if he released Jesus.

Now there was a custom at that time at the annual Passover feast. As a favor to the people, the Roman governor could release one prisoner of their choice. There happened to be in prison a man called Barabbas; with a number of others, he had been arrested for causing a riot that led to a murder.

Now Pilate knew that the chief priests had handed Jesus over to him out of envy. So he thought of a way to free the Savior from their hands. He asked the mob, "Do you want me to release for you the King of the Jews?"

But the chief priests persuaded them to ask for Barabbas instead, so that the whole multitude together cried out: "Away with this man, and give us Barabbas! Not this man, but Barabbas!"

Pilate said to them, "Then what will I do with the man you call King of the Jews?"

And they all cried out again, "Crucify Him! Crucify Him!"

Pilate said, "Why? What evil has He done?"

But they only cried out the louder, "Crucify Him! Crucify Him!"

Jesus Is Scourged, Mocked, and Condemned

Then Pilate ordered his soldiers to take Jesus away and to scourge Him. They led Him into the court of the palace, calling together the whole battalion. Then they stripped Him of His garments, bound Him to a pillar, and scourged Him with cruel whips.

Next they put a purple cloak on Him and, making a crown of thorns, they placed it on His head, with a reed in His right hand. They mocked Him by kneeling before Him and shouting, "Hail, King of the Jews!" They spat on Him and, taking the reed out of His hand, they struck His thorn-crowned head.

At last, Jesus was brought back before Pilate. When he saw Him clothed in a purple robe, crowned with thorns, and covered with blood and filth, he led Him out to the people and said to them, "Behold the Man!"

But the sight of Jesus failed to move the people and the chief priests to pity. Instead, they cried out all the more, "Crucify Him! Crucify Him!"

Pilate said, "Take Him yourselves and crucify Him, because I find no guilt in Him."

But the Jewish leaders said, "We have a law; and according to this law, He must die, because He made Himself out to be the Son of God."

When Pilate heard this, a great fear came on him. Taking Jesus, he led Him back into the palace again and asked Him, "Where do You come from?" But Jesus gave him no answer.

Pilate said, "You won't speak to me? Don't You know that I have the power to crucify You, and I have the power to release You?"

Jesus answered, "You would have no power at all over Me unless it were given to you from above. Those who have handed Me over to you have the greater sin."

Pilate decided to speak to the religious leaders to make

one more effort to have Jesus released. But they wouldn't listen to him. They said, "If you release this man, you are no friend of Caesar. For everyone who makes himself a king sets himself against Caesar."

When Pilate heard these words, he submitted to the will of Our Lord's enemies, because he was afraid they would report him to the Roman emperor. He sat down in the judgment seat that was placed in the square of Gabbatha. Then he took water, washed his hands before the people, and said, "I'm innocent of the blood of this righteous man. See to it yourselves."

A roar went up from the people, and they answered, "His blood be on us and on our children!"

Pointing to Jesus, Pilate said to the people, "Behold your king!"

But they cried out, "Away with Him! Away with Him! Crucify Him!"

Pilate asked, mocking them, "Should I crucify your king?"

But the chief priests answered, "We have no king but Caesar!" So Pilate released to them Barabbas and ordered Jesus to be crucified.

CHAPTER 16

Christ Is Crucified, Dies, and Is Buried

Jesus Takes His Cross

Crucifixion was the Roman way of putting criminals to death. Hanging, strangulation, beheading, burning, and stoning were the methods used by the Jews. But when the Jews came under the power of Rome, the right to inflict capital punishment was taken away from them. They could put someone on trial, and if they found him deserving of the death penalty, the Roman governor would pronounce sentence. Then it was carried out in the Roman way.

At a sign from Pilate, the soldiers led Jesus away. First, they took the purple cloak from His shoulders. His body was bruised and torn and bleeding from the cruel scourging. With rough hands they dressed Him again in His own clothes. Then they placed a cross on His shoulders and led Him away to be crucified.

The sad procession wound its way from the praetorium through the crowded streets, toward one of the gates of the city. Once there, it would follow the road that led to a low hill called *Golgotha*. This name means "place of the skull." On this hill, also known as *Calvary* from the Latin word for "skull," crucifixions took place.

Two other unfortunate men were to be put to death that day. They were criminals found guilty of robbery. Four Roman soldiers walked by the side of each prisoner. They carried the nails and tools that would be used in the crucifixion, and they had orders to stand guard near the cross until the victim was dead and to prevent anyone from trying to rescue him.

At the head of the procession rode a *centurion*, a Roman officer in charge of a hundred soldiers. He carried the wooden boards on which was written the name of each condemned man and the crime he had committed. From time to time, as they went along, the centurion would proclaim this information in a loud voice to the crowds that lined the streets.

Jesus Makes His Way to Calvary

It was now about nine o'clock on Friday morning. Jesus had had nothing to eat or drink since the Paschal supper the evening before. He had suffered terribly during His agony in the garden, and after that had followed a night of horror.

He had been beaten in the house of the high priest, dragged roughly through the streets to Pilate, and scourged and crowned with thorns. He had suffered intense pain and lost a great quantity of blood. The cross weighed heavier and heavier on His shoulders as He walked, and no doubt He stumbled several times beneath its load.

Seeing how weak our blessed Savior had become, the four soldiers who were guarding Him feared that He would die before He reached Golgotha. A man was coming into the city from the country. His name was Simon, and he was from Cyrene. The soldiers grabbed him and forced him to carry the cross behind Jesus.

The news that Jesus had been condemned to be crucified spread throughout the city. A mob of people followed the procession, and as it passed through the city, people came out of their houses or gathered in crowds at the street corners. Many in the crowd were friends of Jesus, and many others, when they saw Him, were filled with compassion.

A number of women were weeping loudly. Turning toward them, Jesus warned them of terrible days to come. "Daughters of Jerusalem," He said, "don't weep for Me, but weep for yourselves and for your children."

According to an ancient tradition, somewhere along this sorrowful journey Jesus came face to face with Mary, His mother. Though the Gospels say nothing about this, it seems more than likely that it really happened, for surely Mary would not be far from Jesus at a time like this. In fact, we do know from the Gospels that once He was crucified, Mary was at the foot of the cross.

Tradition also tells us that a holy woman, named Veronica, came out of her house and offered Jesus a towel with which to wipe the blood and filth from His face. Grateful for this little service, Jesus took the towel from her hands and wiped His face. When He handed it back to her, she saw on it, outlined in blood, the image of His sacred face.

Jesus Is Crucified

At last they reached Calvary. The crosses were laid on the ground, and Jesus and the two thieves were stripped of their clothes.

The Jews had a custom of giving to those about to be crucified a cup of wine mixed with myrrh. This was an act of mercy, for when the victim drank the wine mixed with myrrh, he became drowsy and his sense of pain was deadened. A society of noble ladies had been formed in Jerusalem for the purpose of supplying this merciful drink to all of those who were about to be crucified. But when a soldier offered the wine mixed with myrrh to Jesus, He refused to drink it. Instead, He would drink to the last drop the cup of suffering that His Father had given Him.

Now Jesus was stretched upon the cross, and spikes were driven into His hands and His feet. Ropes may well have been tied around His arms as well, to hold them to the cross. Then they raised the cross and dropped the end of it into one of a number of holes that had been prepared for this purpose. The cross was not very high, the feet of the crucified men being about two feet from the ground.

They placed over the head of Jesus the board that the centurion had been carrying. On it was written His name and the offense for which He had been condemned. Pilate himself had written the title for the cross of Jesus, in Latin, Greek, and Aramaic. It read: "Jesus of Nazareth, King of the Jews."

Meanwhile, the two robbers had been nailed to their crosses as well. One of them was placed on the right of Jesus, the other on His left.

Jesus' Words From the Cross

No sooner had Jesus been raised on the cross than He opened His mouth in prayer. "Father, forgive them," He said, "for they don't know what they're doing."

Yet even during His agony, the enemies of our Savior did not spare Him. Many who passed by mocked Him, wagging their heads and saying, "You who would destroy the Temple and in three days rebuild it, save Yourself! If You're the Son of God, come down from the cross!"

"He saved others," they said sarcastically, "but He can't save Himself. He's the king of Israel, so let Him come down now from the cross so we can believe in Him. He trusted in God; let God deliver Him now. For He said, 'I am the Son of God.'"

The soldiers also mocked Him, saying, "If You're the king of the Jews, save Yourself!"

Meanwhile, someone had told Annas and Caiaphas what Pilate had written on the board over the cross of Jesus. Immediately, they went to him and said, "Don't write, 'The King of the Jews,' but that He said, 'I am King of the Jews.'

But Pilate answered, "What I have written, I have written."

It was the custom for the soldiers guarding a crucified man to divide his clothes among themselves. They disposed of Our Lord's outer cloak, belt, and sandals. But when they came to His tunic, which had been woven in one piece without a seam, they were puzzled. If they attempted to divide it, they would destroy it. So they decided to cast lots to see who would keep it.

In this way the words of the psalmist were fulfilled, who wrote: "They divide My garments among them, and for My clothing they cast lots."

All this time, the Pharisees and the members of the Sanhedrin continued to heap insults on our blessed Savior. When they heard that Pilate had refused to change the title on the cross, they became all the more bitter. They were afraid that the people might think that Jesus had some right to be called the king of the Jews. So they sought to show that they, the leaders of the people, who knew better than anyone else, were convinced that He was not king of the Jews.

One of the robbers who was hanging on a cross beside Jesus began to curse and swear at Him, saying, "If you're the Christ, save Yourself and us!" But the other robber rebuked him.

"Have you no fear of God?" he asked. "We've received the just punishment for our deeds; but this man has done no wrong."

Then he said to Jesus, "Lord, remember me when You come into your kingdom."

"Truly, I tell you," Jesus replied, "this day you will be with Me in paradise."

Jesus' Mother at the Foot of the Cross

The friends of Jesus had forsaken Him. They didn't dare come near the foot of the cross, where the Pharisees and chief priests were gathered. They were afraid something might happen to them.

But there were four disciples who weren't afraid. Boldly they pushed their way through the crowd and stood beside the cross. These were Mary, the mother of Jesus, and her sister; John, the disciple whom He loved; and Mary Magdalene.

Looking down from the cross, Jesus saw His mother and His beloved disciple, gazing up at Him in compassion and love. Tenderly He spoke to Mary. "Woman," He said, "there is Your son."

Then He said to John, "There is your mother."

John understood what Jesus meant. This was the Savior's dying legacy to him and to all people until the end of time. In the hour of death, Jesus gave to us His greatest treasure on earth, His mother. From that moment on, John took her as his own mother.

Jesus Dies

It was about noon when Jesus was nailed to the cross. About that time it grew dark, as though a great storm were coming, and the darkness continued for three hours. It was almost three o'clock when Jesus cried out with a loud voice, *"Eli, Eli, lama sabachthani!"* That means, "My God, my God, why have You abandoned Me?"

Some of those standing around heard this, and they misunderstood. They thought Jesus was calling for the prophet Elijah. But instead, He was quoting from a psalm in the Scripture that had foretold His death.

A moment later, Jesus said, "I'm thirsty."

One of the soldiers took a sponge, filled it with vinegar, and put it on a reed. Then he went up to Jesus and held the sponge against the lips of the dying Savior. But some of the others tried to stop him, saying, "Wait. Let's see whether Elijah will come to save Him."

Jesus had refused the wine mixed with myrrh, because He didn't want His sufferings to be made easier. Now He drank the vinegar offered to Him, so that He might suffer all the more. Again, He would drink to the last drop from the chalice of suffering that His Father had prepared for Him.

At last Jesus said, "It is finished." Then with a loud voice He cried out, "Father, into your hands I commit My spirit." And bowing His head, He died.

At once, frightful things began to happen. Inside the city, the veil of the Temple was torn in two, from the top to the bottom. If it had been torn from the bottom to the top, someone might have claimed that human hands had torn it. But instead, it had been torn by the hand of God Himself.

The earth quaked, and great rocks were broken into pieces. The graves opened. The dead came out of their tombs.

When the centurion who had charge of the crucifixion saw all of this, he was terrified. Striking his breast, he said, "Truly this man was the Son of God." The crowd, too, was filled with awe, and they hurried back to Jerusalem, striking their breasts in anguish.

Evening was approaching, and the Sabbath day was at hand. Not wishing the crucified men to remain on the cross over the Sabbath, the chief priests asked Pilate to have their legs broken. That way they would die more quickly, and their bodies could be taken down from the cross and buried before the Sabbath began.

The soldiers took clubs and broke the legs of the thieves who were crucified with Jesus. But when they came to Jesus, they saw that He was already dead, so they had no need to break His legs. But one of the soldiers took a spear and pierced His side, and immediately there came out blood and water.

Jesus Is Buried

There was a man named Joseph, of Arimathea, a city of Judea. Although he was a member of the Sanhedrin, he was in secret a disciple of Jesus. Before now, he had been afraid to profess his faith openly. But now he went boldly to Pilate and asked him for the body of Jesus.

Pilate was surprised to hear that Jesus was dead so soon. He sent for the centurion, and when he found out from him that, in fact, Jesus was dead, he gave the body to Joseph.

Joseph took the body of Jesus down from the cross and wrapped it in fine linen that he had brought for that purpose. But this time he had been joined by Nicodemus, the one who first came to Jesus by night. Nicodemus brought with him a mixture of myrrh and aloes, about a hundred pounds in weight.

Together they brought the body of Jesus to a new tomb that belonged to Joseph. It had been carved out of a rock not far from Calvary. They placed the body in the tomb, together with the spices, according to the burial custom of the day. Then they rolled a great stone across the door of the tomb and went home.

Mary Magdalene, along with some other women who had followed Jesus from Galilee, stood by and watched while all this was going on,

The following day, the chief priests and Pharisees went to Pilate and said, "Sir, we remember how that imposter said while He was still alive, 'After three days I will rise again.' So command that His tomb be guarded until the third day. Otherwise, His disciples might come to steal away His body, and say to the people, 'He is risen from the dead.' Then the last deception will be worse than the first."

Pilate said to them, "Take a guard of soldiers. Go make it as secure as possible." So the chief priests went to Jesus' tomb, sealed the stone, and set guards to watch it.

CHAPTER 17

The Proof of Christ's Divinity

The Disciples Find the Empty Tomb

The Sabbath at last was over. The first rosy glow of the dawn could be seen in the east, announcing that it was Sunday, the first day of the week. Suddenly, there was a great earthquake, and an angel of the Lord descended from heaven.

He rolled back the stone and sat on it. His face was brilliant like lightning and his clothing white as snow. Seeing him, the guards were struck with terror and fell fainting to the ground.

Shortly after sunrise, Mary Magdalene and Mary, the mother of James and Salome, came to the tomb of Jesus, bringing with them sweet spices to anoint the body. On the way they said to one another, "Who will roll away the stone for us from the door of the tomb?" For the stone was quite large, and they knew they weren't strong enough to move it themselves.

When they came to the tomb, however, they saw that the stone had been rolled away already. Entering the tomb, they found that the body of the Lord Jesus was gone. The guards, too, had disappeared.

By this time the apostles had gathered together in the upper room where Jesus had eaten His last supper with them, when he instituted the Eucharist. Knowing this, Mary Magdalene hastened back to the city and found them there. Calling Peter and John aside from the others, she said, "They have taken away the Lord from the tomb, and we don't know where they have laid Him."

In the meantime, Mary, the mother of James and Salome, had been joined by the other women who had been faithful to our blessed Savior. They decided to look into the tomb again. When they did, they saw what appeared to be a young man sitting on the right side, clothed in a white robe. They were astonished.

He said to them, "Don't be afraid. You seek Jesus of Nazareth, who was crucified. He is risen; He's not here. Look at the place where they laid Him.

"But go, tell His disciples and Peter that He goes before you into Galilee. There you'll see Him, just as He told you."

Hearing this, the women fled from the tomb, trembling with fear and joy. They hurried to Jerusalem to tell the apostles. But the words of the women sounded like idle tales to the apostles, and they didn't believe them.

Peter and John had left the upper room when they heard from Mary Magdalene that the body of Jesus had disappeared. They ran to the tomb, with John outrunning Peter and arriving there first. Stooping down, he looked inside and saw the linen cloths. But he didn't go into the tomb, because he was waiting for Peter.

A moment later Peter came up, and together they went in and saw the linen cloths, along with the napkin that had been tied around Jesus' head. It wasn't lying with the linen cloths, but apart, folded up. When they saw this, both of them believed that He had risen from the dead. So they returned to the other apostles and told them what they had seen.

Jesus Appears First to Mary Magdalene

A little later, Mary Magdalene returned to the tomb and stood at the door waiting. Stooping down, she looked inside and saw two angels in white, sitting there on the stone where the body of Jesus had been laid. One sat at the head, and one at the feet.

They said to her, "Woman, why are you weeping?"

She replied, "Because they have taken away my Lord, and I don't know where they have laid Him."

Straightening up again, she turned around and saw Jesus standing there, but she didn't recognize Him. He said to her, "Woman, why are you weeping? For whom are you searching?"

Thinking it was the caretaker of the garden, she said to Him, "Sir, if you've taken Him from here, tell me where you've laid Him, and I'll take Him away."

Jesus said to her, "Mary."

Then she recognized Him. Falling down at His feet, she said, "Teacher!"

Jesus said, "Don't hold on to Me, because I've not yet ascended to My Father. But go to My brothers, and say to them: 'I'm ascending to My Father and to your Father, to My God and your God.'"

Then He disappeared. She stood up and hurried to Jerusalem to find the apostles. "I've seen the Lord!" she told them. Then she repeated what He had said to her.

The Guards Are Bribed to Lie

The guards who had watched over the tomb finally recovered from the fright that had come over them at the sight of the angel. They fled to Jerusalem and told the high priest everything that had happened. The high priest at once called the Sanhedrin together.

These new developments could cause them great difficulties. The council had to decide what should be done. They voted to give a great sum of money to the soldiers on condition that they would tell the people the disciples of Jesus came by night and stole His body while they were sleeping.

At first the guards hesitated. They were afraid that Pilate would hear of it and punish them for their negligence in going to sleep. They could be executed for having deserted their post.

But the chief priests told them they would explain everything to Pilate and take care of the whole matter. So they took the money and left. After that, they spread the story among the people that the soldiers had fallen asleep, and the apostles had come and stolen the body of Jesus.

Jesus Appears on the Road to Emmaus

Early on Sunday morning, two of the disciples of Our Lord left Jerusalem and set out for Emmaus, a town about seven miles away. As they walked along, they talked of all that had happened since Thursday night. Their hearts were sad as they tried in vain to understand why it was that Jesus, in whom they had believed so sincerely, had come to such a terrible end.

As they were going along, they met a stranger who asked if he could walk with them. It was Jesus, but they didn't recognize Him. "What's this you're talking about as you walk?" He asked. They stood still and looked downcast.

One of them, whose name was Cleopas, answered, "Are you the only visitor to Jerusalem who doesn't know what's happened there the past few days?"

He asked, "What happened?"

They said, "We're talking about Jesus of Nazareth, a prophet, mighty in work and word before God and all the people. Our chief priests and princes handed Him over to be condemned to death, and He was crucified. But we were hoping that He was the One who would redeem Israel.

"Yes, and besides all this, today is the third day since these things took place. Certain women from among us astounded us. They went to the tomb before dawn but couldn't find His body.

"They came back saying that they had seen a vision of angels who said that He's alive. Some of our people went to the tomb and found that what the women said was true. But they didn't find Jesus."

Then Jesus said to them, "You foolish men, slow of heart to believe all that the prophets have spoken! Didn't the Christ have to suffer these things before He could enter into His glory?" Then, beginning with the Books of Moses and all the prophets, He explained all that the Scriptures had foretold about Him.

At last they drew near the town where they were going. Saying goodbye, Jesus started to go on farther. But they urged Him to remain with them, saying, "Stay with us, because it's getting towards evening, and the day is almost done now." So He went with them into Emmaus.

While He was at the table with them, He took bread, blessed it, broke it, and gave it to them. Our Lord was actually celebrating the Eucharist with them. At that moment their eyes were opened so that they recognized Him. But He vanished from their sight.

Their hearts filled with wonder, and they said to each other, "Weren't our hearts burning within us while He was speaking on the road, and explaining to us the Scriptures?" Then, getting up at once, they hurried back to Jerusalem.

There they found the eleven apostles gathered in the upper room, together with a number of other disciples of our Savior. Seeing Cleopas and his companion, the apostles greeted them with the words, "The Lord is risen indeed, and has appeared to Simon."

Then the two who had been to Emmaus told them all about what had happened on the journey, and how they had recognized Him in the breaking of the bread in the Eucharist.

The Sacrament of Reconciliation Is Instituted

Late into the night, the apostles and the others remained in the upper room, talking about the wonderful things that had happened. They had locked the doors for fear that some agent of the chief priests and Pharisees might find them out.

Suddenly, Jesus stood among them and said, "Peace be to you."

They were startled and panic-stricken, because they thought they were seeing a ghost. But He said, "Why are you disturbed, and why do doubts arise in your hearts? See My hands and feet, and know that it's I Myself. Feel Me and see, for a ghost doesn't have flesh and bones, as you see that I have."

Having said this, He showed them His hands and feet. But even though their hearts were filled with joy, they weren't quite sure He could actually be Jesus. So He asked, "Do you have anything here to eat?"

They offered Him a piece of broiled fish and a honeycomb. And when He had eaten some of it in their presence, He took what remained and gave it to them.

Now they were sure that it was Jesus, and not a ghost. Then He said, "Peace be to you. As the Father has sent Me, I also send you." When He had said this, He breathed on them, and said, "Receive the Holy Spirit. If you forgive the sins of any, they are forgiven; if you retain the sins of any, they are retained."

In this act, Jesus gave to His apostles and their successors, the bishops, the authority to forgive sins on His behalf. The bishops share this authority with priests, and they exercise this authority in the Sacrament of Reconciliation.

Jesus Helps Thomas to Believe

Now Thomas, one of the apostles, wasn't with the others that night when Jesus came. When he returned the next day, they told him how they had seen the Lord. But he said, "Unless I see in His hands the print of the nails, and put my finger into the place of the nails, and put my hand into His side, I won't believe."

Eight days later, they were assembled again in the upper room. This time, Thomas was with them. The doors were shut, but Jesus came and stood among them and said, "Peace be with you." Then, going up to Thomas, He said, "Put your finger here, and see My hands; and stretch out your hand here, and place it in My side. Don't be faithless, but believing."

Thomas answered, "My Lord and my God!"

Jesus replied: "Because you've seen Me, you've believed. Blessed are those who have not seen, and yet have believed."

Jesus Appears by the Sea of Galilee

At the command of our blessed Savior, the apostles left Jerusalem and went back to Galilee. One day not long after, Simon Peter, Thomas, Nathanael, James, John, and two others were standing together on the shore of the Sea of Galilee. Peter said to the others, "I'm going fishing."

They said, "We're coming with you." And they went out and climbed aboard the boat.

All night long they labored, but they caught nothing.

When morning had come, they rowed toward the shore. They were still some distance out when they saw a man standing at the water's edge.

He called out to them, "Children, do you have any fish?"

They answered, "No."

Then He said to them, "Cast the net on the right side of the boat, and you'll find them."

They did as He directed, and they caught so many fish that they weren't able to draw in the net; it was too heavy.

Seeing this, John said to Peter, "It's the Lord!" At once, Peter put on his clothes and jumped into the water, swimming for the shore. The other apostles came in the boat, dragging after them the net with the fish in it.

When they got to land, they saw a charcoal fire with fish laid on it, as well as some bread. Jesus said to them, "Bring here some of the fish you've just caught."

Simon Peter went aboard and hauled the net to shore. Though it was full of large fish—one hundred and fifty-three of them—the net wasn't broken.

Jesus said to them, "Come and eat!" Then they all sat down on the ground with Him, and He served them the bread and the fish and ate with them. None of them dared ask Him, "Is it really You?" because they knew for certain it was the Lord.

Jesus Gives Peter Instructions

When they had finished eating, Jesus took Peter aside. The apostle had denied Jesus three times. Now the Savior would give him the chance to affirm His love for Him three times. He would also make it clear that Peter would have the primary responsibility to care for Our Lord's flock.

Jesus said to Peter, "Simon, son of John, do you love Me more than these?"

Peter answered, "Yes, Lord, You know that I love You."

Jesus replied, "Feed My lambs."

A moment later, Jesus said to him again, "Simon, son of John, do you love Me?"

Peter said, "Yes, Lord, You know that I love You."

Jesus said, "Feed My lambs."

A third time, Jesus said, "Simon, son of John, do you love Me?"

Peter was grieved that Jesus had asked him the third question, and he said, "Lord, You know all things; you know that I love You."

Then Jesus said, "Feed My sheep. Truly, truly, I tell you, when you were young, you fastened your own belt and walked wherever you wanted to walk. But when you're old, you'll stretch out your hands, and someone else will fasten your belt for you, and lead you where you don't want to go."

By these words our blessed Savior prophesied that the words Peter had spoken at the Last Supper would one day come true. He would go to prison and death for the Savior, being crucified for His sake.

Jesus then said to Peter, "Follow Me." As Peter was walking along with Jesus, he turned and saw John, the disciple Jesus loved, following in the distance. He said to Jesus, "Lord, what about this man?"

Jesus said to him, "If I want him to remain until I come, what's that to you? You follow me!"

These words of our Savior gave rise to a rumor among the apostles that John wouldn't die. But Jesus didn't mean that John wouldn't die. He meant instead that John wouldn't die a martyr's death.

The Commission of the Apostles

Jesus commanded the eleven apostles to meet Him on a certain day on a mountain in Galilee. When they arrived there, they saw Jesus waiting for them. Kneeling down, they worshipped Him.

Jesus said to them, "All authority in heaven and on earth has been given to Me. So go and make disciples of all nations, baptizing them in the name of the Father, and of the Son, and of the Holy Spirit, and teaching them to observe everything that I have commanded you.

"And behold, I am with you always, even to the end of the world."

Jesus Ascends Into Heaven

It was now forty days since Jesus had risen from the dead. Once more the apostles were gathered together at the table with Jesus. He commanded them not to leave Jerusalem, but to wait there for the coming of the Holy Spirit, whom He had promised to send.

"John baptized with water," He said, "but you will be baptized with the Holy Spirit, not many days from now."

Even at this point, the apostles didn't fully understand that the kingdom of Jesus was not of this world. They asked Him, "Lord, will You now restore the kingdom to Israel?"

But He said to them, "It's not for you to know the times or the dates that the Father has determined by His own authority. But you'll receive power when the Holy Spirit comes on you, and you'll be witnesses for Me in Jerusalem, and in all Judea and Samaria, and even to the ends of the earth.

"Everything written about Me in the Law of Moses, and in the prophets, and in the psalms, must be fulfilled. It is written that the Christ must suffer, and on the third day rise again from the dead; and that penance and the forgiveness of sins must be preached in His name to all nations, beginning at Jerusalem.

"You are witnesses of these things. And I send the

promise of My Father on you. But stay in the city until you're clothed with power from on high."

Then He led them out of the city toward Bethany. When they came to the Mount of Olives, He blessed them, and while they were looking at Him, He was lifted up, and a cloud took Him out of their sight.

They stood gazing into the sky, hoping to catch one last glimpse of Him. Then suddenly they saw two angels standing beside them in white clothing, who said, "You men of Galilee, why do you stand looking up into heaven? This Jesus who was taken up from you into heaven will come back in the same way you've seen Him go into heaven."

Then they worshipped Jesus and went back to Jerusalem with great joy in their hearts, praising and blessing God.

Matthias Takes the Place of Judas

The upper room, where Jesus had eaten with them the Last Supper, now became the home of the apostles. There the eleven of them were gathered together: Peter and John; James and Andrew; Philip and Thomas; Bartholomew and Matthew; Simon and James, the son of Alpheus; and Jude, his brother. The Blessed Virgin Mary was with them, and Mary Magdalene, and the other faithful women who had ministered to Him during His life here on earth. Other disciples and followers of our Savior came to the upper room each day, and all of them spent the time together in prayer.

One day, when about a hundred and twenty of them were present, Peter stood up among them and told them that the time had come to appoint a successor to Judas Iscariot, so that there would once again be twelve apostles. He suggested that they choose some disciple who had been with Jesus from the baptism of John until the day of His ascension, so that he could be a witness, with the other apostles, of Our Lord's resurrection.

Two names were suggested: Joseph, also called Barsabbas, who was surnamed Justus; and Matthias.

Then all knelt down, and Peter prayed: "You, Lord, knows the hearts of all. Show us which of these two You've chosen to take the place in this ministry and the apostleship from which Judas has fallen away by his sin."

Then they cast lots, and the lot fell to Matthias. From that time on, he was numbered among the apostles.

These twelve, along with Mary and the other disciples, continued their long vigil of prayer and hope in the upper room. They had full confidence that Jesus would send the Holy Spirit on them, filling them and clothing them in power, just as He had said. A few days later, Our Lord kept His promise in a glorious way.

PART FOUR

How the Apostles Became the Foundation of the Church

CHAPTER 18

The Growth of the Early Church

Jesus Sends the Holy Spirit

The Feast of Pentecost had begun, and Jerusalem was filled with visitors who had come to celebrate this joyful festival of the first fruits. In the upper room, the apostles and the other disciples of our blessed Savior were gathered together, united in prayer. Suddenly there came a sound from heaven, like a mighty wind, and it shook the whole house where they were assembled.

Tongues of fire appeared to all those in the room and settled on each of them. They were all filled with the Holy Spirit. Then they began to speak in foreign languages that they had never learned, as the Holy Spirit prompted them to speak. It was the fulfillment of Jesus' promise to them: God's Spirit, the Advocate, had come to clothe them with power to be witnesses to all they had seen and heard.

The crowds who clogged the streets of the city included devout Jews from many nations. The noise of the great wind was heard all over the city, and crowds came running together to surround the house where the disciples were staying.

There they witnessed a wonderful sight. The twelve apostles were standing on the rooftop, preaching to the multitude. And a great excitement came on the people, because every person in the crowd heard them speak in his own language.

They said with amazement, "Aren't all these who are speaking Galileans? So how is it that can we listen to them speak, each of us in the language we've spoken since we were born? . . . We've heard them speak in our own languages the wonderful works of God."

Some of the listeners were perplexed and asked, "What does all this mean?" But others claimed that the apostles were drunk and babbling. Then Peter stood up and began to preach.

Peter's Pentecost Sermon

"Men of Judea and all you who live in Jerusalem: Let this be known to you, and listen to my words. These men aren't drunk, as you think; it's only nine o'clock in the morning!

"What's happening has fulfilled what was spoken through the prophet Joel: 'And it will come to pass in the last days, says the Lord, that I will pour out My Spirit on all people; and your sons and your daughters will prophesy, and your young men will see visions, and your old

men will dream dreams. . . . And it will come to pass that whoever calls upon the name of the Lord will be saved.' "

Peter knew that many in his audience had witnessed Jesus' death, and some had even sought it. Now he addressed them directly.

"Men of Israel, hear these words. Jesus of Nazareth was a man approved by God among you by miracles and wonders and signs, which God did through Him in your midst, just as you yourselves know. This Jesus, handed over according to the definite plan and foreknowledge of God, you have crucified and killed by the hands of wicked men.

"But God has raised Him up, having freed him from the sorrows of death. For it was not possible for Him to be held by it. . . . Of this we all are witnesses. Exalted at the right hand of God, and having received from the Father the promise of the Holy Spirit, He has poured out this Spirit that you see and hear. . . .

"Let all the house of Israel know with all certainty, then, that God has made this Jesus whom you crucified to be both Lord and Christ!"

When the people heard these words, they were pierced to the heart with remorse. They said to Peter and to the other apostles, "Brothers, what shall we do?"

Peter replied, "Repent and be baptized, every one of you, in the name of Jesus Christ, for the forgiveness of sins. And you will receive the gift of the Holy Spirit. For to you is the promise, and to your children, and to all who are far away—even to all those whom the Lord our God calls to Himself. . . . Save yourselves from this crooked generation!"

Peter's Pentecost sermon was powerful and inspired by the Holy Spirit, who was working in the hearts of his listeners. Those who accepted Peter's message were baptized and became part of the newborn Church. That day alone, about three thousand people were converted. In a new and powerful way, the Feast of Pentecost had shown itself to be the feast of first fruits—the first great harvest of souls into the Church.

The Fervor of the Early Christians

The early Christians lived their faith with great joy and commitment. They gathered faithfully to pray, to hear the teaching of the apostles, and to celebrate the Eucharist. They watched in trembling amazement as God performed miracles in Jerusalem through the hands of the apostles, just as He had worked through Jesus. Sometimes the sick were healed just by having Peter's shadow fall on them while he was walking by!

All the believers showed a generous charity, inspired by the Holy Spirit, through sharing what they owned. Whatever they didn't need, they sold, and then distributed the money to those who were in need. They met at the Temple and in their homes to worship and have fellowship.

The love and joy of these early Christians made a deep impression on their neighbors. The people respected them and wanted to know why they lived the way they did. As a result, each day more people were coming to believe in Jesus, receive baptism, and become part of the Church.

A Lame Man Is Healed

One morning Peter and John went to the Temple to pray. On their way, they met a man who couldn't work for a living because he had been unable to walk all his life. His friends were carrying him to sit at the gate of the Temple known as the Beautiful Gate. He usually sat there each day, asking people for alms as they passed by on their way to pray.

When the lame man saw the two apostles, he asked them for alms to help him. But Peter and John gazed at him and said firmly, "Look at us." So he fixed his attention on them, hoping to receive some money from them. But he was in for a big surprise!

"I have no silver or gold," Peter said, "but what I do have, I'll give you: In the name of Jesus Christ of Nazareth, get up and walk!" Taking him by the right hand,

Peter pulled the man to his feet. The man felt healing strength flow into his legs, so he jumped up and began to walk around.

Imagine his great joy! He joined Peter and John as they entered the Temple, and though it must have looked strange to everyone watching, he kept jumping up and down and praising God for his healing. The people who had seen him begging alms for many years were amazed to see him cured, for he was more than forty years old.

Peter and John Are Arrested

The man stayed close to Peter and John, grateful for what they had done. Because of the excitement, a crowd began to gather on the porch of the Temple. So Peter took the opportunity to preach to them.

"Men of Israel," he shouted, "why are you amazed at this? Why do you stare at us as if we had made this man walk by any power or holiness of our own? . . . The God of Abraham, and the God of Isaac, and the God of Jacob, the God of your fathers, has glorified His Son Jesus. . . .

"You killed the Author of life, but God has raised Him up from the dead; of that, we are witnesses. And it is His name, by means of faith in His name, that has made strong this man you see and recognize. And it is the faith that comes through Jesus that has given him the perfect health you now see.

"And now, brothers, I know that you in acted in ignorance, and your rulers did as well. . . . So repent and be converted, so that your sins can be blotted out. . . . God has raised up His Son and sent Him first to you to bless you, so that all of you can turn from your wickedness."

While Peter was speaking, some priests, some Sadducees, and an officer of the Temple arrived. They didn't want anyone preaching about Jesus, so they had Peter and

John arrested. In the meantime, however, many of their listeners had come to believe in Jesus through what Peter had said.

After being held in jail overnight, Peter and John were brought the next morning before the chief priests. They demanded to know by what authority Peter had been preaching. Peter was filled with the Holy Spirit and responded with words similar to what he had preached in the Temple.

The chief priests were amazed at Peter and John's boldness, especially because they knew that the two apostles were fishermen without the kind of training that religious teachers were expected to have. They also knew that the lame man had been healed in the presence of many witnesses. So they knew they couldn't deny that the miracle had taken place.

The chief priests withdrew to a private room to discuss how to handle the situation. They finally decided to warn Peter and John not to speak about Christ any more. So they summoned the two apostles and commanded them not to teach in the name of Jesus.

Peter and John replied to them: "You can decide for yourselves whether it's right in God's sight for us to listen to you rather than to God. But we must speak about what we've seen and heard."

The chief priests didn't dare to punish the two apostles, because they feared the people, who were praising God for healing the lame man. So they threatened them again and let them go. But Peter and John returned to their friends, thanked God for their release, and asked Him to help them preach with even greater power and boldness than before. When they had all prayed together, the building where they had gathered shook with the power of the Holy Spirit, who filled them again.

The Apostles Are Arrested Again

The apostles continued to preach publicly with great boldness. The high priest and the Sadducees were filled with jealousy, because so many people no longer looked to them for spiritual leadership, but looked to the apostles instead. Because the Sadducees had opposed Jesus, they were losing their status and influence in the city.

Finally, they arrested Peter and John again, along with the other apostles who were preaching, and put them in jail. But during the night, an angel of the Lord opened the doors of the prison and let them out. The angel told them: "Go, stand and speak in the Temple to the people all the words of this new life."

The apostles returned to the Temple and began preaching at daybreak. Not realizing that the prisoners were free, the chief priests assembled the elders and the Sanhedrin, then ordered that the prisoners be brought to them. But when the officers arrived at the jail, they couldn't find the apostles in their cell. So they returned to the council with this report:

"The jail was in fact securely locked, and the guards were standing in front of the doors. But when we opened their cell, no one was inside."

The council was perplexed and wondered what they should do. But just then a messenger arrived, saying, "Look! The men you put in prison are standing in the Temple and teaching the people!" So they sent officers to arrest them again, but without violence, because they feared that the people might try to stone them if they hurt the apostles.

When the officers arrived with the apostles, the apostles were stood before the Sanhedrin for questioning. The high priest said sternly, "We strictly ordered you not to teach in this name. But look! You've filled the whole city of Jerusalem with your teaching, and you want to make us guilty of this man's blood!"

Peter and the other apostles replied boldly: "We must obey God rather than men. The God of our fathers raised Jesus, whom you put to death. . . . Now God has exalted Him at His right hand to be Prince and Savior, to grant repentance to Israel and forgiveness of sins. And we are witnesses to these things, and so is the Holy Spirit, whom God has given to all those who obey Him."

At these words, the members of the council were cut to the heart. They wanted to kill the apostles! But one of them spoke up, a Pharisee named Gamaliel who was a teacher of the Law and respected by all the people. He instructed that the apostles be taken outside so that he could address the council.

"Men of Israel," he said. "Be careful about what you do with these men. . . . I say to you, keep away from them and leave them alone. If this plan or this undertaking is simply a work of human beings, it will fail. But if this movement is of God, you won't be able to overthrow them. You might even find yourselves fighting against God!"

The council agreed with Gamaliel. So they called in the apostles and had them scourged. Once more they ordered them not to speak in the name of Jesus, and then they released them.

The apostles went their way. Despite their pain from the scourging, they were overjoyed that God had counted them worthy to suffer disgrace for the name of Jesus. Not even for a single day did they stop preaching and teaching in the Temple, and from house to house, the good news of Jesus Christ.

The First Deacons

In those days the number of new Christians was increasing daily. But there were already divisions developing in the community that caused tensions, especially between the Jewish converts who spoke Greek—called the *Hellenists*—and those who spoke Aramaic, called the *Hebrews*. The Hellenists were complaining that the Hebrews were neglecting their widows when the community distributed food to the needy each day.

So the Twelve called together all the disciples and announced that new leaders were needed to administer the distribution of food. This way, the apostles could focus on teaching, providing the sacraments, and governing the new Church, while the new leaders could focus on feeding the needy and other practical responsibilities. They wanted the community to choose seven men for this role, with a good reputation and full of wisdom and the Holy Spirit.

The disciples agreed that this was a necessary step to take for a growing community. So they chose Stephen, a man full of faith and of the Holy Spirit; and also Philip, Prochorus, Nicanor, Timon, Parmenas, and Nicolaus. When these men were brought before the apostles, they prayed for the men and laid hands on them.

These men were the first deacons of the Church. They served the people under the leadership of the apostles, and as they did, the Church in Jerusalem continued to grow in numbers. Many of the Temple priests came to believe in Jesus and entered the Church. And the word of God went out to all the city.

CHAPTER 19

The Seed of God Is Scattered

Stephen, the First Christian Martyr

The new deacon Stephen was full of grace and power, teaching and working great miracles among the people. Some of the people who hadn't become Christian began disputing with him. But they couldn't withstand the wisdom of the Holy Spirit who spoke through him.

To silence Stephen, they bribed some men to say that they had heard him speaking blasphemy against Moses and against God. These accusations stirred up the people and their religious leaders. They seized Stephen and brought him before the Sanhedrin.

Just as it had been in the trial of Jesus, false witnesses were brought forward. They accused Stephen of speaking against the Temple and the Law of Moses. The high priest asked, "Are these things true?" Then Stephen began to address the assembly, and his face looked like the face of an angel.

Stephen preached a powerful defense of his faith. He began by recalling for his listeners the long history of God's chosen people, and all that God had done for them. He reminded them how often their forefathers had turned away from the Lord, misunderstood His message, and even killed His messengers, the prophets.

Finally, he concluded with a stinging rebuke to the Sanhedrin, which had cooperated in having Jesus put to death: "You always oppose the Holy Spirit, just as your forefathers did! Which of the prophets did they fail to persecute? They killed those who foretold the coming of the Righteous One, the One you yourselves have betrayed and murdered! You honor the Law as delivered by angels, yet you don't obey it!"

When the council heard this rebuke, they were cut to the heart and began an uproar against Stephen. But Stephen looked up to heaven and declared that he saw the glory of God, with Jesus standing at the right hand of God's throne. The council refused to listen, but instead put their hands over the ears and rushed on him as a mob.

They dragged Stephen outside the city and stoned him. Those who were throwing the stones had to take off their cloaks to do it. A young man named Saul was standing there watching, approving of their actions, so they left their cloaks with him for safe keeping.

While they were stoning Stephen, he prayed aloud, "Lord Jesus, receive my spirit!" Then falling on his knees, he cried out with words that echoed what His Master had said upon the cross: "Lord, don't hold this sin against them." With these words, he died.

That same day, a great persecution of the Christians broke out in Jerusalem. Many had to flee the city for their lives. But wherever they went, they talked about Jesus, and through them, faith in Him began to spread.

The New Faith Spreads to Samaria

You may recall how Jesus met the woman at the well in Samaria, and how that meeting led to an opportunity for other Samaritans to meet Him and believe in Him. Jesus had commanded His disciples to preach, not only in Judea, but also in Samaria and in the lands beyond. So Our Lord's disciples returned there to bear witness to the Savior and to establish the Church.

The deacon named Philip went to Samaria and began to preach and work miracles. He healed people who were crippled and paralyzed, and he cast out demons from those who had been plagued by them. Many people came to faith through his ministry, were baptized, and entered the Church. Their joy was known throughout the city.

A man named Simon had been practicing sorcery in Samaria, claiming to be a great magician, and calling himself "the Power of God." Many people had been deceived by his performances. He too came to believe, and after he was baptized, he began to follow Philip around.

In the meantime, word came to the apostles in Jerusalem that many Samaritans were believing the gospel. So they sent Peter and John to them. The Samaritan believers had been baptized, but they hadn't yet received the Holy Spirit as the believers in Jerusalem had done on the day of Pentecost.

Peter and John laid hands on the new believers, and the Holy Spirit came down on them. The new convert Simon was among those who received the Holy Spirit. He had been awestruck by the miracles that Philip had worked, and now he marveled to see how the Spirit came down on the believers when the apostles laid hands on them.

The apostles soon discovered that Simon's heart was not in the right place. It seems as if his conversion may have been motivated by a desire to perform great marvels as Philip and the apostles did. He offered them money, saying, "Give me this power, too, so that anyone on whom I lay my hands can receive the Holy Spirit."

Peter replied, "May your silver perish with you, because you thought that the gift of God could be bought with money! You have no part in this matter, because your heart isn't right before God. So repent of this wickedness of yours! Ask God to forgive this intention of yours, because your heart is bitter and bound by sin!"

Simon was frightened. He said soberly, "Pray for me to the Lord, so that nothing of what you've said will happen to me."

After preaching and teaching the people about Jesus, the apostles returned to Jerusalem, preaching in Samaritan villages on their way back. But God had other plans for Philip the deacon.

Philip and the Ethiopian

An angel of the Lord spoke to Philip, saying: "Get up and go south to the desert road that runs from Jerusalem to Gaza." So Philip obeyed.

Once he was on that road, he saw a man from the African nation of Ethiopia, who served the Ethiopian queen and was in charge of her treasury. Though the man may have been a Gentile, he was returning from Jerusalem, where he had gone to worship at the Temple. He was sitting in his chariot, reading the book of the prophet Isaiah as his driver guided the horses.

The Holy Spirit told Philip to go talk to the Ethiopian, so he ran up to the chariot and greeted him. When Philip heard that the man was reading the words of a Jewish prophet, he asked, "Do you understand what you're reading?"

The man replied, "How can I, unless someone explains it to me?" Then he asked Philip to get in the chariot and sit with him.

The Ethiopian was reading one of the passages from Isaiah that foretold the coming of Jesus. He asked Philip whether the prophet was speaking about himself or someone else. Philip was never one to miss a chance to talk about Jesus. So he started preaching the gospel to the Ethiopian, beginning with this scriptural passage.

Before long, the Ethiopian was convinced that Jesus

had come as the Savior of the world. As the chariot continued along the road, it came near a body of water. "Look!" the Ethiopian said, "here's some water. What's to keep me from being baptized?" Then he ordered the chariot to stop.

The two men went down into the water, and Philip baptized him. But when they came up out of the water, the Spirit of the Lord took Philip away. The Ethiopian never saw him again, but he was overjoyed as he went his way.

Philip, meanwhile, suddenly found himself, through a miracle of God's power, in the Gazan city of Azotus. Passing through the area, he preached the gospel to all the cities where he traveled.

Peter Visits the Churches

In time, the persecution of the Christians in Jerusalem died down. Throughout all Judea, Galilee, and Samaria, the Church was at peace. The new Christians were strengthened as they lived in reverence for God and with encouragement from the Holy Spirit.

Peter, as the leader of the Church, went out to visit the Christians living in various cities and towns. When he came to the city of Lydda, he found a man named Aeneas, who had been paralyzed and confined to his bed for eight years. Peter said to him, "Aeneas, Jesus Christ heals you. Get up and make your bed."

Immediately, Aeneas got up. All the people in Lydda and the nearby town of Sharon found out what had happened, and they believed in the gospel.

In the city of Joppa there was a disciple of Jesus named Tabitha, which means "gazelle." She was known for devoting herself to good works and acts of charity. But it happened at this time that she fell ill and died. So her body was prepared and laid out for her funeral.

Since Lydda was near Joppa, the disciples heard that Peter was there and sent two messengers asking him to come without delay. So Peter went back with them to Joppa, and they took him to the room where her body had been laid. All the local widows who had been blessed by Tabitha's kindness were there weeping in grief, and they showed Peter all the clothes that Tabitha had made for them.

Peter asked everyone to leave the room. Then he knelt beside Tabitha's body and prayed. Finally, he turned to her and said, "Tabitha, get up."

The woman opened her eyes, saw Peter, and sat up. He called her friends back into the room, and gave her back to them alive.

News of the miracle spread all through the city of Joppa. Many people came to believe in Jesus, and Peter stayed there some time to minister to them. He was staying in the home of a man named Simon, who made a living by turning animal hides into leather.

Peter Meets Cornelius

At that time there was a man in Caesarea named Cornelius. He was a Roman centurion, but he had come to believe in the one true God worshipped by the Jews. He and his entire family were fervent in their faith, praying often and giving to the poor.

About nine o'clock one morning, Cornelius had a vision of an angel from God who called his name. The centurion was terrified, and he replied, "What is it, Lord?"

The angel said, "Your prayers and your alms have ascended to God, and He remembers them. Now send men to Joppa to find a man named Simon, also called Peter. He's staying with Simon the tanner, who lives by the seaside."

After the angel departed, Cornelius called two of his servants, along with another soldier who also worshipped God. He told them the whole story and sent them to Joppa.

The next day about noon, as the men were approaching the city, Peter went out to pray on the roof deck of the home where he was staying. He grew hungry, so he began preparing something to eat. But suddenly, he saw a vision of heaven opened, and something like a great sheet was let down by its four corners from heaven to the earth.

In the sheet were a multitude of insects, birds, and four-footed animals. Then came a voice, saying, "Get up, Peter; kill and eat." But Peter objected. Many of the creatures in the sheet were unclean according to the Law of Moses, so Jews were forbidden to eat them.

The voice spoke to Peter a second time, telling him not to reject the creatures God had made. The words were repeated three times. Then the sheet was taken back up into heaven.

Peter was perplexed by the vision. The Law of Moses, which God had given the Jewish people, had forbidden them to eat certain animals or to have meals with Gentiles. These animals and peoples were considered unclean. The laws had intended to keep the Jewish people separated from those who didn't share their faith, so that the Jews weren't tempted to act and think the way the Gentiles did.

Now God seemed to be telling Peter through this vision that the time for observing such laws was finished. The avoidance of certain foods, which required the avoidance of social dealings with Gentiles, was no longer necessary. In the Church, God was bringing Jews and Gentiles together as one people in Christ.

The vision had come just in time. As Peter stood

pondering its meaning, the men sent by Cornelius arrived at the door of the house, asking for him. The Holy Spirit told Peter that they had come, and that he must go down and return with them to their home, without any hesitation, because God had sent them.

So Peter went down from the roof deck and told them he was the man they were seeking. When he asked why they had come, they told him about Cornelius' vision, and what the angel had said to him. So Peter invited them in and they had a meal together. The apostle now understood that as Christians, Jews were no longer to avoid eating with Gentile Christians or otherwise remaining separate from them. They were all one in Christ.

Cornelius Becomes a Christian

The next day, Peter, the messengers, and a few of the disciples from Joppa set out together for Caesarea. When they reached the city, Cornelius was waiting for them, along with several relatives and close friends he had gathered together in his home. As Peter entered the house, Cornelius met him and fell at his feet as if to worship him.

But Peter pulled him up to his feet, saying, "Get up! I myself am also just a man." Then he went with Cornelius to the room where the people were gathered, and he began to speak to them.

He reminded them that according to the old laws, it wasn't permitted for a Jew to associate with a Gentile or to visit him in his home. But God had told him not to consider Gentiles unclean anymore. So here he was in a Gentile home, and he wanted to know exactly why Cornelius had sent for him.

Cornelius replied by telling about his vision of the angel and his obedience to the angel's instructions. He noted his gratitude to Peter for coming, then he asked the apostle to tell the gathering whatever the Lord instructed him to say. Peter was happy to fulfill his request.

"Now I really understand that God shows no partiality," the apostle said. "In every nation, anyone who reveres Him and does what's right is acceptable to Him." Then Peter began preaching to those assembled the good news of Christ's kingdom, just as he had preached to the Jews in Jerusalem on the Day of Pentecost.

While Peter was preaching, the Holy Spirit came on those who were listening to him speak. The Jewish believers who had come with Peter from Joppa were astounded. They heard Cornelius and his Gentile family and friends speaking in tongues and praising God, just as the Jewish believers had done at Pentecost. God was bringing both the Jews and the Gentiles to faith in His beloved Son!

Peter asked, "If these people have received the grace of the Holy Spirit just as we did, how can we possibly refuse to baptize them?" Then he instructed that they be baptized in the name of Jesus Christ. Afterward, the new believers were eager to hear more about the kingdom of God, so Peter stayed with them a few days to teach them.

Word of what had happened at Joppa got back to the disciples in Jerusalem. Many were overjoyed that the Jews weren't the only ones who were receiving the word of God. But others worried that Peter was disobeying the old laws by associating with Gentiles.

Peter had to explain to them what had happened. He recounted his vision, the visit of the messengers right afterward, and his preaching to the Gentiles in Joppa. Once he told them how the new Gentile believers had received the Holy Spirit just as they themselves had received Him, they realized that God's will was to bring Jews and Gentiles together as one in the Church. So they praised God for His grace.

Meanwhile, in other cities as well, Gentiles were coming to faith in Christ. At the great city of Antioch in Syria, for example, where there were many Jewish residents, the new believers who had scattered from the persecution in Jerusalem became witnesses both to Jews and to Gentiles. A great multitude was added to their numbers there, and it was in Antioch that the disciples were first called "Christians."

Peter in Prison

Back in Jerusalem, King Herod had decided to persecute the Church. He had James the brother of John killed with a sword, and when he saw that this action brought him favor with some of the Jewish religious leaders, he proceeded to arrest Peter as well during the Feast of Passover. Then Herod had Peter thrown into a prison cell, carefully guarded by sixteen soldiers.

Herod intended to put Peter on trial before the people when the Passover festival was over. But the Church was praying constantly and fervently for Peter, and God heard their prayers.

The night before Peter's trial, he was bound in two chains, sleeping between two soldier guards, with sentries posted outside the door of his cell. An angel of the Lord appeared and stood beside him, and a light filled the room. Then the angel tapped Peter on the side to wake him.

The angel said to Peter, "Get up quickly." The chains fell off his hands. "Put on your clothes and sandals," the angel said. Peter sleepily obeyed. Finally, the angel said, "Now wrap your cloak around you and follow me."

Peter followed him out of the prison. But he wasn't sure whether he was having a vision, or the angel was real. They passed through the first and second guard and came to the iron gate that led into the city. It opened to them on its own, without anyone touching it.

Peter and the angel went out, then passed on through one street. Immediately the angel left him. Finally Peter came to himself and realized that the Lord had actually sent an angel to rescue him from Herod.

Once Peter realized his situation, he went to the house of a disciple named Mary, whose son was named John Mark. Many of the believers were gathered there, praying for Peter. When he knocked on the outer gate, a maid came to answer it.

As soon as she heard Peter's voice, she was so overcome with joy that she ran to tell the others—without first opening the gate to Peter! She announced to them that Peter was standing at the gate, but they told her she was crazy. Some even speculated that it was Peter's guardian angel.

But Peter kept knocking, and eventually they opened the door and saw him standing there. They were amazed and began talking all at once, but Peter waved to them to be quiet so he could tell them how the Lord had rescued him from prison. Then he instructed them to tell the other apostles, and he left.

When the morning came, the soldiers were confused and fearful, debating how Peter could possibly have escaped while under such heavy guard. Herod was furious. When a search for Peter proved fruitless, the king had the guards executed.

The Church Continues to Grow

Herod's arrogance and brutality knew no bounds. But he was soon rewarded for his wickedness. One day he dressed in his finest royal attire, sat in his judgment seat, and began speaking to the people.

To gain his favor, they began shouting, "It's the voice of a god, not of a man!" But rather than telling them that he was no god, he enjoyed their false praise. Immediately, an angel of the Lord struck him down, and he died a horrible death, being eaten inside by parasites.

But the word of the Lord continued to spread as more and more people came to believe the gospel. Obeying the command of our blessed Savior, the apostles and other disciples of Jesus now went out into the whole world to preach the Gospel. As our Savior had promised them, they had the power to work miracles, which helped to convince people that God was with them, and that their message was true.

The apostles ordained priests, who were called *presbyters* (or elders), to assist them in their ministry, along with deacons such as Stephen and Philip. They consecrated bishops who would be their successors and carry on the work of the Church after their death. With this leadership, the number of those who believed in their preaching grew constantly.

At first the apostles preached to the Jews. But as we have seen in Joppa and Antioch, they went out to the Gentile nations as well, and they made great numbers of converts. In this way the Church of Christ began its mission here on earth. Like the mustard seed of which our Savior had spoken, it grew from small beginnings until it became the great institution that today continues to spread throughout the world, preaching the Gospel to every creature.

Among those who preached the gospel to the Gentiles, one of the most famous and successful was Paul the Apostle. But Paul actually started out as a violent enemy of the Church. So God had to act in a powerful and unusual way to convince him that Jesus Christ was truly the Lord and Savior of the world.

CHAPTER 20

Paul's Conversion and Early Ministry

The Conversion of Saul

The young man named Saul, who witnessed the stoning of Stephen and approved of it, became a ferocious enemy of the new Christians. Once Stephen was dead, Saul began to devastate the Church, entering house after house of the believers and dragging them away to prison.

Not content with persecuting the Christians of Jerusalem, he went to the high priest. Saul then asked him for letters to introduce him to the Jewish synagogues in the great Syrian city of Damascus. He certainly had the credentials to earn their respect: He was a strict Pharisee from the city of Tarsus in Asia Minor, trained in Jerusalem by the famous rabbi Gamaliel. Saul was also a Roman citizen by birth, and like many Jews of his day, he went by a second, Latin name as well, which was Paul.

The letters Saul received authorized him to search for Christians in Damascus and bring them back in chains to Jerusalem. As he journeyed, he issued constant threats of murder against them. But as he approached the city, a blinding light from heaven suddenly shone down on him.

Saul fell to the ground in terror. Then a voice said to him in Hebrew, "Saul, Saul, why do you persecute Me?"

He replied, "Who are you, Lord?"

"I am Jesus of Nazareth," the voice answered, "whom you are persecuting."

"What should I do?" Saul asked.

"Get up and go into the city," came the reply, "and you'll

be told what to do. For I have appeared to you for this purpose: to appoint you to serve and bear witness to what you have seen, and to the visions you will have of Me, when I deliver you from the people and from the Gentiles.

"I send you to them to open their eyes. I want them to turn from darkness to light, and from the power of Satan to God, so that they can receive forgiveness of sins and a place among those who are sanctified by faith in Me."

The brilliant light had blinded Saul. So the men who were with him had to take him by the hand and lead him the rest of the way into Damascus. For three days, he couldn't see, and he spent the time in prayer and fasting.

Saul and Ananias

Now there was in Damascus a disciple named Ananias. The Lord Jesus appeared to him in a vision, calling his name.

"Here I am, Lord," Ananias replied.

"Get up," the Lord said, "and go to a street named Straight. Ask at the house of Judas for a man of Tarsus named Saul. He's praying there, and he has seen in a vision a man named Ananias come in and lay his hands on him so he can regain his sight."

Ananias was frightened when he heard these words. "Lord, I've heard from many people about this man," he objected, "and how much evil he's done to the disciples in Jerusalem. And here in Damascus he has authority from the high priest to arrest all who call on Your name."

But the Lord answered, "Go! For this man is My chosen instrument. He will carry My name before the Gentiles and kings and the sons of Israel, and I will show him how much he must suffer for the sake of My name."

So Ananias went to the house of Judas. He found Saul there, and he laid hands on him with these words:

"Brother Saul, the Lord Jesus who appeared to you on your journey has sent me, so that you can recover your sight and be filled with the Holy Spirit."

Immediately, something like scales fell from Saul's eyes, and he recovered his sight. Then Saul got up and was baptized. Finally, he took some food and regained his strength.

Saul Begins Preaching

For many days afterward, Saul remained in Damascus. Right away he began to preach that Jesus was the Son of God in the same Jewish synagogues where before, he had hoped to find Christians to persecute. Those who heard him were amazed: How could the same man who had done such harm to the Church in Jerusalem, and who had planned to arrest the Christians in Damascus, now be a preacher of Christ?

As a Pharisee who had trained under one of the great rabbis of his time, Saul knew the Scriptures well. He used that knowledge now to show how Jesus fulfilled many prophecies of the Jewish prophets. He explained how the new gospel message fit into the age-old plan of God.

Saul's opponents weren't able to refute his arguments showing that Jesus was the promised Messiah. So they plotted to kill him. They guarded the city gates day and night so they could abduct him and assassinate him.

But Saul received word of their plot. So his Christian brothers disguised him and took him in the night to the city wall. They lowered him down, outside the wall, in a great basket, and he escaped.

Saul returned to Jerusalem, but the Christians found it hard to believe that he had actually become one of them. They feared that he was trying to trick them into revealing themselves. But a man named Barnabas, who was influential in the Church at Jerusalem because of his preaching and holiness, acted as Saul's sponsor.

Barnabas told the apostles Peter and James how Saul had been converted. He bore witness to Saul's effective preaching in Damascus. So Saul was accepted into the Christian community, and he began preaching boldly about Jesus in Jerusalem as well.

Saul's preaching was powerful. But once again, his opponents plotted to kill him. So the disciples smuggled him out of the city and down to Caesarea, then finally back to Tarsus.

Paul's First Missionary Journey

Some time later, Barnabas was serving the Christians in the great Syrian city of Antioch. He went to Tarsus looking for Saul, and when he found him, he brought him back to Antioch. For a year they worked together there, teaching the people and bringing new converts into the Church.

One day when the Christian leaders there were praying and fasting to seek God's will, the Holy Spirit said to them: "Set apart for me Saul and Barnabas for the work to which I have called them." The leaders laid hands on the two men to set them apart for the ministry. Then they sent them out on their new mission as apostles to both Jews and Gentiles in the lands where they would preach.

Their journeys took them far and wide. They ministered on the island of Cyprus, in the Mediterranean Sea, and in several cities of Asia Minor. Usually they would begin a mission by preaching in the local synagogue, if there was one, so that the local Jewish population would have the chance to believe first. Then they would go out and preach to the Gentiles as well.

Saul was now going by his other name, Paul, perhaps because a Latin name would be more popular among the

Gentiles. He worked miracles, just as Jesus and the other apostles had done. Again, the power of God that was displayed through these wonders helped to convince people that the gospel message was true.

When Paul and Barnabas preached in the city of Lystra, they met a man who had been crippled all his life. He listened intently to Paul's preaching. The apostle could tell that the man had the faith to be healed, so he said to him, "Stand upright on your feet." And he jumped up and began to walk around.

The crowds saw what had happened. They believed in the gods of the Greeks, so when they saw such power displayed, they cried out, "The gods have come down to us in the likeness of men!" They thought Barnabas was the Greek god Zeus, and Paul, the Greek god Hermes.

The local priest of Zeus brought oxen and flowers, prepared to sacrifice to the apostles as gods. But when they heard this, Paul and Barnabas rushed out into the crowd.

"Men, why are you doing this?" they shouted. "We are mortal human beings like you. But we bring you the good news that you should turn from these empty things to the living God who made heaven and earth and the sea, and everything in them."

Then they explained that even though they couldn't see their Creator, He had given them all the gifts of the earth as a testimony to His love for them. But even with these words, they could hardly restrain the crowds from offering sacrifices to them.

Before long, some Jewish opponents of the Christian teaching came from Antioch and another city. They convinced the crowds to reject the apostles' message. The mob stoned Paul. Next they dragged him outside the city, because they thought he was dead. But after the mob dispersed, the disciples gathered around Paul, and he stood up again. Then they all returned to the city.

The next day Paul and Barnabas set out for the city of Derbe. They preached there, then returned to the cities where they had already preached, encouraging the disciples there to be faithful to Christ despite the persecution they suffered. In each town, they consecrated priests for the local church with prayer and fasting.

After visiting a few more towns, Paul and Barnabas returned to Antioch at last. There they called the Christians together and reported all that God had done in bringing the Gentiles to faith in Jesus. In this way Paul concluded his first missionary journey.

The Council of Jerusalem

About this time, some Jewish believers came from Judea to Antioch and began preaching that the Gentile Christians couldn't be saved unless they observed all the Law of Moses. Paul and Barnabas opposed this teaching. So the church at Antioch decided to send these two apostles, along with some other representatives of the community, to Jerusalem. They intended to take up the matter with the apostles and priests there.

When they arrived, they were welcomed by the Christians at Jerusalem. Their reports of so many Gentiles believing in Jesus was received as good news. But some of the Jewish believers who had been Pharisees still insisted that the Gentile Christians must observe all the Law of Moses.

The apostles and priests called a council to discuss and resolve this issue. After a long debate, Peter stood up in the assembly to speak. He recalled what had happened with Cornelius and his family and friends. God had shown Peter in a vision that these Gentiles should be accepted into the Church, and when they believed, they were baptized and received the Holy Spirit in the same way as the apostles on the Day of Pentecost.

Peter concluded: "God, who knows the heart . . . made no distinction between us and them, but cleansed their hearts by faith. So why do you now try to put God to the test by putting a yoke on the neck of these disciples that neither our forefathers nor we ourselves have been able to bear? But we believe that we are saved through the grace of the Lord Jesus, just as they are."

The assembly became silent as they considered his words. Then Barnabas and Paul told about all the great miracles God had worked through them among the Gentiles in the cities where they had preached.

Finally the Apostle James stood to speak. He affirmed Peter's words and explained how the coming of the Gentiles into the Church was a fulfillment of God's plan as foretold in Scripture. He advised that they require the Gentile Christians only to observe certain moral commands of the Law of Moses, which were timeless and universal. He also noted that they should avoid anything that had been associated with the worship of idols, because they were false gods that led people astray from the true God.

The entire council agreed. They sent representatives to the church at Antioch, who returned with Paul and Barnabas to instruct the Christians there about their decision. They declared that the judgment had been made by them under the direction of the Holy Spirit. And when the church at Antioch received their instruction, they were delighted with the encouragement that it gave them.

CHAPTER 21

Paul Takes the Gospel to Europe

Paul's Second Missionary Journey

Paul and Barnabas remained at Antioch for some time, teaching and preaching the word of the Lord, along with many others. Then they decided to set out on new missionary journeys. Barnabas took a young disciple named John Mark and set out for Cyprus. Paul chose a man named Silas, a prophet and teacher who had been chosen by the apostles at Jerusalem to bring the council's message to Antioch.

In this second missionary journey, Paul and Silas set out for other cities where the apostles had earlier preached. They encouraged the disciples there and reported the decision of the council at Jerusalem. Under the leadership of these two missionaries, the number of believers increased in these cities daily.

In the city of Lystra lived a young disciple named Timothy. Timothy's father was a Gentile, but his mother was a Jewish Christian. He was highly regarded by the Christians there. So Paul chose this young man to accompany them on their further journeys.

This little missionary band had plans to preach in several more cities of Asia Minor. But the Holy Spirit prevented them from carrying out those plans. Instead, the Spirit gave Paul a vision one night to direct them. In it, a man from Macedonia, a land north of Greece, stood pleading, saying, "Come over to Macedonia and help us."

Paul Comes to Philippi

So Paul concluded that God had called them to preach in Macedonia, and they set sail for that province. They arrived in Philippi, the leading city of Macedonia and a Roman colony. It was the apostle's first missionary effort on the continent of Europe.

One Sabbath morning, the missionaries went down to the riverside. Since there was no synagogue in Philippi, they were hoping that Jewish residents of the area would gather there for prayer. Sure enough, they found some women praying there, and they joined them.

Paul began to preach about Jesus. One of the women listening was named Lydia, a wealthy merchant who sold cloth for royal courts. She was a Gentile who had come to believe in the one true God, so she prayed with the Jewish believers.

The Lord opened Lydia's heart to receive Paul's message. So she and her whole household were baptized. Then she convinced the missionaries to stay in her home.

One day as they were on their way to pray, a young slave girl met them. She was possessed by a demon, who helped her practice fortunetelling. Her masters made a great profit from her practice.

The girl followed Paul and the others around, crying

out, “These men are servants of the Most High God, and they proclaim to you a way of salvation!” Though her words were true, she was causing a commotion, and people probably thought she was hired to promote the missionaries. So Paul was grieved by what she was doing.

After days of putting up with her behavior, Paul finally turned to her and commanded the demon, “I order you in the name of Christ to leave her!” It left her that very moment.

Now the girl's masters realized that their hope of profit from her fortunetelling had fled along with the demon. So they seized Paul and Silas and dragged them into the marketplace, bringing them before the authorities of the city. They protested: "These men are making a great disturbance in our city. They are Jews, and they are advocating practices that it would be unlawful for us to adopt or practice, since we are Romans."

The crowd joined in on the attack. At the rulers' orders, they stripped off the clothes of the two missionaries and beat them with rods. Then, after inflicting many lashes on them, they threw them in prison and ordered the jailer to keep them secure. So he put them in the most secure cell, deep within the prison, and fastened them with chains.

Paul and Silas in Prison

Despite their bleeding backs and chained limbs, Paul and Silas chose to praise God in the prison cell, joyful that they had been considered worthy to suffer for Jesus. They were praying and singing hymns, and all the other prisoners were listening. But at midnight, suddenly a great earthquake shook the foundations of the prison.

All at once, the doors flew open and everyone's chains fell off. The jailer was roused from his sleep, and when he saw what had happened, he assumed that the prisoners had all fled away. He knew that the authorities would have him brutally executed for allowing them to escape, so he took out his sword to kill himself.

But Paul cried out to him the darkness, "Don't harm yourself; we're all here!"

The jailer was deeply moved by the apostles' willingness to remain captive so that his life would be spared. Recognizing the earthquake as a sign that God approved of Paul's preaching, he called for a light, then ran into the cell where Paul and Silas were being held. He knelt before them, trembling with fear, then brought them out, asking, "Sirs, what must I do to be saved?"

The apostles replied, "Believe in the Lord Jesus, and you will be saved, and your household as well." Then he took them right away, in the middle of the night, to his home, and he washed their wounds. They preached the word of the Lord to the jailer and his family, and they were baptized immediately. He set out a meal for the missionaries to eat, rejoicing with all his household over their new faith in God.

The next day, when Paul and Silas had returned to the prison, the rulers sent word that they were to be let go without further public attention. So the jailer invited them to come out and go their way. But Paul knew the rulers had acted illegally: He and Silas were Roman citizens, and according to Roman law, they should not have been mistreated as they had been the day before.

"We're Roman citizens," Paul declared, "yet they have had us beaten publicly and without trial, then chained us in prison. And now they want to let us go secretly? By no means! They can come here themselves to let us out."

When the rulers were told what Paul said, they were alarmed, because they themselves could be punished for what they had done. So they came to the prison and begged them to leave the city. Paul and Silas finally came out of their prison cell and went to Lydia's house, where they had been staying. After meeting with the new Christians there and encouraging them to remain faithful to the Lord, they departed from the city.

Paul in Thessalonica and Beroea

Next Paul and Silas came to the city of Thessalonica, where there was a Jewish synagogue. Following his usual strategy, he preached there first. For three weeks he told them about Jesus and explained how God had fulfilled His promise to the Jewish people to send a Messiah.

Some of the people in the synagogue were persuaded, along with some Greeks who worshipped God. But others were jealous of his influence and rejected his message. So they gathered a mob and attacked the house of a man named Jason, where the missionaries had been staying. They hoped to bring them before the city authorities, but they could find only Jason and a few other disciples there.

They dragged them out and declared to the rulers: "These men who have turned the world upside down have come here, too. Jason has given them lodging in his home. They're acting against the decrees of Caesar, saying that there's another king, Jesus!"

They stirred up the crowd and the rulers against the men. So the authorities demanded that they pay bail and then let them go. That night, the disciples sent Paul and Silas away secretly to the city of Beroea to avoid further trouble.

They had a similar experience in that city, though there were more converts there from the synagogue than before. Many Jews and Gentiles alike came to believe in Jesus. But some of the troublemakers in Thessalonica heard that Paul and Silas were preaching in Beroea, so they came and stirred up a mob to come after them. Silas and Timothy remained in hiding for a while, but Paul went on to Athens, the great city of the Greek philosophers and teachers.

Paul in Athens

In Athens, Paul went to the synagogue to speak to the Jews and the Greek believers in the one true God. But he was disturbed to see how many idols the pagan people worshipped. So he went to the marketplace each day as well to talk about Christ with anyone who would listen.

Some of the pagan philosophers debated with him. They mocked him, saying, "What is this babbler trying to say?" Others insisted, "He seems to be a preacher of strange gods," because he spoke of Jesus and His resurrection.

There was a place in the city called the *Areopagus,* where many people gathered daily to hear the latest news and to debate ideas. Some of the philosophers brought Paul there, saying, "Can you tell us just what is this new doctrine you're teaching? You bring some strange things to our ears, and we want to know what they mean."

So Paul stood up in the Areopagus and began to speak. But since he knew his listeners were educated pagans, unfamiliar with Jewish beliefs about God, he took a different approach from the one he had taken in the synagogue. He started by noting certain beliefs and practices they had, even as pagans, that pointed to the truth about God. By affirming these truths, he found a common ground to stand on with them as he went on to teach about Christ.

Paul observed that the Greek people were extremely religious, worshipping many gods. Then he noted that among all the idols he saw, there was an altar with this inscription: To the Unknown God. "The One you worship as unknown," he announced confidently, "I want to make known to you!"

With that intriguing starting point, Paul went on to talk about the one true God who has created all things. He actually quoted a pagan poet whose name they would have known, saying that all people are God's children, and that "in Him we live and move and have our being." We owe all that we are to Him.

Paul explained that people everywhere try to find their way to this God. But even though He's close to each person, their search for Him may be difficult because they are blinded by sin and ignorance. God has been patient with their search. But now He calls all people to repent of their wayward lives, and to believe in the Man He has appointed to judge the world. To show who this Man is, God Himself raised Him from the dead.

A few of the Greeks in Athens believed Paul's message and became Christians. But most of those who heard him were more interested in playing with new ideas than in taking them seriously. In addition, the Greeks tended to look down on the human body as a prison to be escaped at death. So they were especially scandalized by Paul's claim that just as God had raised Jesus both body and soul from the dead, all people will have their bodies restored to them on judgment day.

Some of the philosophers sneered at Paul's words. Others dismissed him by saying, "Well, we'll hear you speak again sometime about this matter." So Paul concluded his preaching in that city and went on the great city of Corinth.

Paul in Corinth

In Corinth, Paul stayed in the home of two Jewish believers, Aquila and his wife, Priscilla. They were tentmakers, and since Paul had learned that same trade in his youth, he worked with them while he was there. That way, he wouldn't be a financial burden to them.

Meanwhile, Timothy and Silas arrived from Macedonia to join him again. The missionaries preached about Jesus in the synagogue each Sabbath, and they persuaded many of the Jews there, as well as a number of Greeks. But in the end, those who rejected the gospel message were so firm in their opposition that Paul stopped teaching in the synagogue.

Instead, Paul began to teach in a home next door to the synagogue, owned by a Greek who worshipped the true God. The leader of the synagogue joined Paul there and became a Christian as well, along with all his household. Though the opposition was strong, God spoke to Paul one night in a vision.

"Don't be afraid," the Lord said. "Speak and don't be silent. For I'm with you. No one will attack you and harm you, for I have many people in this city."

Paul remained in Corinth for a year and a half, preaching and teaching. The people of the synagogue tried to have the authorities arrest him, but to no avail. The missionaries had great success in the days following, so that a thriving church was established there. Finally they left Corinth and, passing through several other cities, they returned to Antioch, where they had begun. Paul's second missionary journey was complete.

CHAPTER 22

Paul's Third Missionary Journey

Paul in Ephesus

From Antioch, Paul set out on his third missionary journey, the last one recorded in Scripture. He came to the great city of Ephesus, and he found about a dozen believers there. But their formation as Christians was quite limited.

Paul asked them, "Did you receive the Holy Spirit when you came to believe?"

They answered, "We've never even heard that there *is* a Holy Spirit!"

"What kind of baptism did you have?" Paul asked.

"The baptism of John," they replied.

So Paul had to explain to them that John's baptism had prepared the way for Jesus, but it wasn't the same as Christian baptism, which they still needed to receive. So they were baptized in the name of the Lord Jesus. Then Paul laid his hands on them, and the Holy Spirit came on them, so that they spoke in tongues and prophesied.

Next Paul went to the synagogue to teach. For three months he spoke boldly about Jesus, and some believed his message. But others rejected him and denounced the Christian faith. So he and the disciples withdrew from the synagogue and began to teach in a nearby lecture hall. Their ministry continued there for two years, with great success.

While Paul was in Ephesus, he performed extraordinary miracles. The people pressed handkerchiefs and aprons to his body, then carried them away to lay on the sick and demon-possessed. When they did, the sick were healed and the demons were cast out.

Some traveling Jewish exorcists came through town. They were the seven sons of a Jewish high priest named Sceva, and they had heard about the power of the name of Jesus through Paul's ministry. So they decided they would attempt to cast out demons in His name, even though they weren't Christians and didn't know Jesus themselves.

They addressed a demon-possessed man: "I adjure you by the Jesus whom Paul preaches."

But the evil spirit replied, "Jesus I know, and Paul I know. But who are you?"

Then the possessed man leapt at them and violently overpowered all seven of them at once. Terrified, they fled from the house where they were, tattered and bruised.

This event was publicized throughout the city, and fear fell on those who heard about it. The name of the Lord Jesus came to be held in high honor. Many more people came to believe, including those who had practiced sorcery. They collected their books of magic and burned them publicly. There were so many that the price of them altogether was reckoned at fifty thousand pieces of silver.

In this way, the word of the Lord spread powerfully and prevailed.

The Riot of the Silversmiths

Now the city of Ephesus was a great center of worship for the Greek goddess Artemis. A large temple was dedicated to her there. Local silversmiths conducted a profitable business making little silver shrines to her and selling them. And the entire city enjoyed the financial benefits of having so many visitors to the city who came to worship at her temple.

The growing number of Christians in town, however, became a threat to all the commerce related to the pagan goddess. When people turned from idols to the true God, they stopped worshipping Artemis and buying her little silver shrines. So all the craftsmen and tradesmen whose livelihood depended on worshippers of the goddess decided that Paul's preaching had to be silenced.

One silversmith named Demetrius gathered them together and called for action. "Men!" he shouted. "You know that all our wealth comes from this trade. And you can see and hear that not only at Ephesus, but also throughout nearly the whole province of Asia, this man Paul has persuaded many people and turned them away from Artemis, saying, 'Gods made by human hands are no gods at all!'

"There's a danger, not only that this business of ours will be discredited, but even that the temple of the great Artemis will be regarded as nothing. The magnificence of the goddess who is worshipped by all Asia and the whole world will be on the decline."

On hearing this, the crowd became furious, and they began shouting, "Great is Artemis of the Ephesians!" The city was filled with confusion, and they rushed into the public theater, dragging with them two Macedonian men who were travelling with Paul. The apostle himself wanted to go to the theater to address the crowd, but the

Christians kept him from going because they feared what would happen to him there.

Different factions of the mob that had gathered were shouting different slogans all at once. Most of them didn't even know why they were there! For about two hours, people were chanting, "Great is Artemis of the Ephesians!"

Finally, the town clerk came out and quieted the crowd. He assured them that Ephesus would retain its valuable position as the keeper of the temple of Artemis. The Christians hadn't really committed any crimes, he reminded them, so they should remain calm and not do anything rash.

Furthermore, he added, any legal charges or complaints could be brought to the proper courts for settlement. But if the people didn't disperse, they themselves could be punished for rioting. At last the crowd calmed down, and the town clerk sent them all home.

Paul Begins on His Way to Jerusalem

By this time, Paul was convinced that God wanted him to return to Jerusalem. He knew that his reputation as a powerful Christian missionary made it dangerous for him to go there. But he was determined to arrive in Jerusalem in time for the Feast of Pentecost, after he had left Ephesus and made his way through several cities to encourage the Christians there.

Everywhere he went, the believers welcomed him with joy and gratitude for his ministry. In the city of Troas, they gathered with him to celebrate the Eucharist late in the evening in an upper room. He was leaving the next morning, so he had many things to tell them before he left, and his sermon continued until midnight.

A young man named Eutychus was sitting in the window, listening to Paul speak, but feeling drowsy. As the apostle's sermon ran on, poor Eutychus went to sleep at last and fell out of the third-story window to the ground. The people rushed downstairs and found him dead.

Paul also went down to him, laid himself upon him, and embraced him. He said to those around, "Don't be alarmed. There's still life within him." And they led the boy away, alive.

Then Paul and the others returned to the upper room, where they celebrated the Eucharist. He continued to teach them until daybreak, and then he left town.

Paul's Farewell Address

After sailing to several towns, Paul arrived at a place called Miletus, not far from Ephesus. He called the Christian priests of that city to come meet with him before he went on to Jerusalem. When they had assembled, he spoke to them one last time before they would say their last goodbye.

"I'm going to Jerusalem," he said solemnly, "compelled by the Holy Spirit, not knowing what will happen to me there. But in every city I visit, the Spirit warns me through the prophets and others that imprisonment and persecution are awaiting me.

"Even so, I don't count my life to be of any value, nor as precious to me, if only I can finish my course and fulfill the ministry I've received from the Lord Jesus: to bear witness to the gospel of the grace of God.

"Now I know that all you among whom I preached the kingdom will see my face no more. . . . So take heed to yourselves and to the whole flock over which the Holy Spirit has placed you as guardians, to feed the Church of the Lord, which He has purchased with His own blood.

"I know that after my departure fierce wolves will come in among you, and they won't spare the flock. And even from among your own selves, men will arise speaking perverse things, to draw away the disciples after them. So be alert! . . .

"Now I commend you to God, and to the word of His grace, who is able to build you up and give you an inheritance among all those who have been made holy."

Having said this and more, he knelt down and prayed with them. They wept and embraced Paul and kissed him, deeply saddened because he had told them that they would never see him again. Then they brought him to the ship, and he set sail with the others who were travelling with him.

CHAPTER 23

Paul in Jerusalem and Rome

Paul Goes to Jerusalem

Paul and his companions made their way through several more cities on their way to Jerusalem. In Caesarea, on the coast of Palestine, a prophet named Agabus journeyed from Judea to speak to Paul. He approached the apostle, took his belt, bound his own feet and hands with it, and declared, "This is what the Holy Spirit says: The man who owns this belt will be bound by the Jews at Jerusalem, and they will hand him over to the Gentiles."

On hearing this, all Paul's companions begged him not to go to Jerusalem. But Paul replied: "What do you mean by weeping and breaking my heart? I'm ready, not only to be bound, but to die at Jerusalem for the name of the Lord Jesus."

The others couldn't persuade him not to go, so they gave up trying and said, "The Lord's will be done." Then they made preparations to go with him to Jerusalem.

When the missionaries arrived in Jerusalem, they received a warm welcome from the Christians there. But a few days later, some of Paul's opponents saw him in the Temple and stirred up a mob to seize him.

"Men of Israel, help!" they shouted. "This is the man who teaches everyone everywhere against the Jewish people and the Law and this Temple. He's even brought Gentiles into the Temple, desecrating this holy place!"

The whole city was thrown into confusion, and the mob dragged Paul out of the Temple. They were about to kill him when news of the disorder came to the Roman tribune. He ordered centurions and soldiers to accompany him to the place where the riot was happening.

When they arrived, the mob saw the soldiers and stopped beating Paul. The tribune seized him, ordered him to be bound in chains, and asked who he was and what he had been doing. Some in the crowd shouted one thing, and others shouted another. Since he couldn't learn anything in the confusion, he ordered Paul to be taken to the soldiers' barracks.

Paul Addresses the Crowd

As the apostle was about to be taken away, he spoke in Greek to the Roman tribune. The tribune thought he was the leader of an Egyptian revolt, but Paul told him who he really was. When Paul asked him to be allowed to address the crowd, the tribune agreed.

When the apostle began speaking to them in Aramaic, they quieted down. He told them who he was and how he had trained in Jerusalem to become a strict Pharisee. He recalled how he had at first persecuted the Christians, but then described in detail his conversion experience on the road to Damascus.

When he declared that God had commissioned him

to bring the gospel of Jesus to the Gentiles, someone shouted, "Get rid of such a man from the earth! He doesn't deserve to live!" Then the mob became violent again, shouting, throwing dust into the air, and stripping down to get ready to fight.

The tribune ordered him to be taken to the barracks, where he would be scourged and interrogated with torture. But when they had bound him, Paul once again used his Roman citizenship to his advantage. "Is it legal for you to scourge a Roman," he asked a centurion, "and that without a trial?"

The centurion told the tribune, and the tribune was worried that he had broken the law. But he kept Paul in custody overnight, and the next day he called together the priests and Sanhedrin. Then he set Paul in front of the council so he could find out why they wanted to kill him.

Paul Before the Sanhedrin

After a brief and heated exchange with the high priest, Paul addressed the entire assembly. His strategy was brilliant: He knew that the council was composed of both Pharisees and Sadducees, and that these two groups constantly fought over their differences in belief. Pharisees believed in the resurrection of the dead, and also in angels. Sadducees believed in neither.

So Paul made an announcement that was sure to get them fighting: "Brother Pharisees, I'm a Pharisee and the son of a Pharisee. I'm on trial for teaching hope in the resurrection of the dead!" This was of course a true statement, because at the heart of the gospel was the insistence that Jesus had been raised from the dead, and that he would someday raise His followers from the dead.

Paul's strategy worked immediately. An argument erupted among the Sanhedrin. In the resulting uproar, the Pharisees defended Paul, and the Sadducees railed against them. When the dispute turned violent, the tribune feared that Paul would be torn to pieces. So he ordered the soldiers to take the apostle back to the barracks.

The next evening, Jesus appeared to Paul and said to him, "Be strong! Just as you've borne witness to me in Jerusalem, you'll do the same in Rome."

When morning came, forty of Paul's enemies gathered and made a vow that they would neither eat nor drink until they had killed him. Then they conspired with the chief priests and elders, telling them to request from the tribune a new opportunity for the Sanhedrin to examine Paul. When Paul was being brought to appear before the council, they would lie in wait, then ambush the soldiers and murder him.

News of their plot came to the tribune by way of Paul's young nephew. So the tribune had Paul taken out of the city by an armed escort in the middle of the night, and sent him to the Roman governor Felix in the city of Caesarea.

Paul on Trial

The governor held Paul until the high priest and some others came from Jerusalem to make their case against him. First they praised the governor to try to curry favor with him. Then they accused Paul of causing disorders and rebellions wherever he went.

The apostle gave a spirited defense, insisting that the charges against him were false. Felix postponed judgment on the case, and later asked Paul to speak privately to him and his Jewish wife about Jesus. When Paul began speaking about justice, self-control, and judgment day, Felix became uncomfortable and said he would hear more at a later time.

But the governor had no intention of listening to the apostle preach again. He was actually hoping that Paul would bribe him to be released. But Paul refused to do such a thing, so he remained in prison for two years.

After Felix was succeeded as governor by a man named Festus, the new governor ordered Paul to appear before him to be examined. Once again the Jewish religious leaders from Jerusalem came to make their accusations, and once again the governor was not convinced that Paul was guilty. Finally, when it was suggested that Paul return to Jerusalem to be tried by the Sanhedrin, he exercised his right as a Roman citizen, and appealed his case to Caesar.

Festus ordered that Paul be brought to Rome for trial before a Roman court. But first he had the apostle brought before King Agrippa, whose father, King Herod, had ordered the Apostle James to be executed. Agrippa and his sister, Bernice, were curious about what Paul was preaching.

Yet one more time, Paul told the story of his conversion and his mission journeys, all the way up to the present moment. But when he concluded with the declaration that Christ had risen from the dead to bring salvation to the world, Festus cried out, "Paul, you're crazy! All your great learning has driven you crazy!"

"I'm not crazy, excellent Festus," Paul replied. "I'm just speaking the truth." Then he asked Agrippa, who embraced the Jewish faith, whether he believed what God had promised through the prophets.

Agrippa replied, "You think you'll persuade me in a short time to become a Christian!"

Paul answered, "Whether short or long, I would to God that not only you, but also everyone else who hears me today, could become as I am—except for these chains!"

Festus, Agrippa, and Bernice then withdrew to a private room to discuss Paul's case. They agreed that he had done nothing to deserve death or even imprisonment. But Paul had appealed to Caesar, and so Festus still had to send him to Rome.

Paul Is Shipwrecked

Soon Paul and the other prisoners were turned over to a centurion named Julius, who was to guard them on their voyage to Rome. But the winds weren't in their favor, and they spent many days at sea on a series of ships without making much progress. Before long, winter was approaching, and Paul warned the centurion and the ship's crew that it was too dangerous to continue, because of winter storms. When they stopped on the island of Crete, he advised them to remain in harbor there for the winter.

But they rejected his advice and set sail again. Soon afterward, a violent wind developed, which drove the ship off course. As they were tossed about by the furious storm, to lighten their load they first threw some of the cargo overboard, and then some of the ship's gear as well.

For days, storm after storm raged. The clouds were so thick that neither the sun by day nor the stars by night were visible. As the ship was tossed about, the crew and passengers began to lose all hope that they would survive.

Then Paul stood up among them and said, "Men, you really should have listened to me. If we had stayed at Crete, you would have been spared this disaster and loss.

"Even so, now I beg you to take heart. Though the ship will be lost, no lives will be lost. For last night, an angel came to me from the God I belong to and serve. He stood by me and said, 'Don't be afraid, Paul! You must stand before Caesar at Rome. And God has granted to you the lives of all those who are with you.'"

After two weeks, the storms had ended, but the ship was adrift. One night about midnight, the sailors determined that they were near land. Fearing that they might be dashed against the rocks, they planned to escape on a small boat, abandoning the soldiers and prisoners to their fate. But Paul learned of their plans and told the centurions and soldiers, who stopped the sailors from leaving the ship.

Sure enough, despite their best efforts, the next day the ship was wrecked when it struck a shoal some distance from the beach. Stuck in the sand, the ship was pounded furiously by the waves, and it broke apart.

The soldiers wanted to kill the prisoners to keep them from swimming to shore and escaping. But the centurion stopped them. He ordered all who could swim to jump overboard first and get to land. The rest paddled to shore on pieces of debris from the ship. Just as the angel had promised Paul, everyone made it safely to land.

Paul on the Island of Malta

Soon they learned that the island where they had been shipwrecked was called Malta. The natives of the island showed their visitors great kindness. They lit a fire to warm them because it had begun to rain, and they were cold.

When Paul gathered a bundle of sticks to lay them on the fire, a viper crawled out of them to escape the heat. It bit him, fastening its teeth in his hand. When the natives saw this, they said to one another, "This man must be a murderer. Even though he escaped the sea, justice won't allow him to live."

Paul shook off the snake into the fire without suffering any harm. The natives were expecting him to swell up from the venom and suddenly fall down dead. But after waiting a long time and seeing that he was unhurt, they changed their minds. He must be a god, they said!

The ruler of the island, a man named Publius, lived on a large estate nearby. When he found out about the shipwrecked men, he took them all in and entertained them graciously for three days. As it turned out, his hospitality was richly rewarded.

It happened that the father of Publius was sick with fever and dysentery. So Paul went into his room, laid hands on him, and prayed for him. Immediately the old man was healed.

When news spread around the island about what Paul had done, everyone who was sick came to him, and he healed them all. They honored the apostle and his companions with many gifts. And when they started to set sail three months later, their hosts provided them with everything they needed.

Paul Arrives at Rome

Finally Paul and the other prisoners arrived at a port near Rome. The Christians of the city heard that he had come, so they traveled to meet him on his way to the city. When Paul saw them, despite his chains and the difficulties that awaited him, he gave thanks to God and was greatly encouraged.

After they came into the city, the apostle was spared another prison term. Instead, he was placed under house arrest. The authorities allowed him to live by himself with a soldier to guard him.

Paul soon invited the leading Jewish men of Rome to gather at his home. When they assembled, he explained to them that he had done no wrong, and that he was being persecuted by the religious leaders in Jerusalem for preaching that God had sent the promised Messiah. They replied that they hadn't heard of any charges made against him personally, but many Jews they knew were speaking against the new Christian faith.

The apostle went on to preach to them the goods news of Jesus Christ. As it had happened in every other place where he preached, some believed, and some did not. But over the next two years, he continued to preach boldly to all those who came to visit him.

The Deaths of the Apostles

At this point, the biblical story of Paul comes to a close. Some ancient traditions say that he made a fourth missionary journey, to Spain and other lands. However he may have spent his final years, the earliest records of the Church agree that in the end, he was beheaded by the Roman emperor Nero for being a Christian. That method of execution was usually reserved for Roman citizens, so one last time, Paul's Roman citizenship played an important role in his story.

In the same persecution of the Church, we're told, Peter was executed in Rome for his faith as well. He was not a Roman citizen, so he was crucified. But he was placed on the cross upside down, because he told his executioners that he didn't deserve to die as Jesus had died.

One by one, all the other apostles except John died a martyr's death for their Lord as well. Each was killed in a foreign land where he had boldly and heroically preached the gospel. Though John wasn't put to death, he was persecuted and endured many trials because of his faith. But God allowed him to live to an old age, perhaps so he could care for Jesus' mother and also write, late in life, the Gospel that bears his name.

Even after the apostles were gone, however, the Church was able to continue and grow strong. Christ had provided new leaders through the appointment of bishops to be the apostles' successors. This *apostolic succession,* as it's called, continues even today, with an unbroken chain of bishops stretching all the way back to the time of Our Lord.

The Writing of the New Testament Books

We can be grateful to God that the faith of the apostles, and the Church for which they became the foundation, still live on. In addition to laying the groundwork for the Church, some of these faithful men, along with their associates, wrote the works that have become the New Testament of the Bible. In that way, and through the Church's sacred Tradition, they continue to speak God's word to the people of every generation.

One of Paul's fellow missionaries, a physician named Luke, wrote the Gospel that bears his name. In addition, he composed what we now call the Book of Acts, the first history of the Church. The Gospels of Matthew, Mark, and John also come to us from the apostles and their companions.

Some of the letters the apostles wrote to the first Christians are included in the Bible as well. These *epistles,* as they are called, helped the early believers—and still help believers today—to understand more about God; His divine Son, Jesus Christ; the Church that He established; and the way to live faithfully the teaching of Our Lord.

Certain details in the epistles also add to our knowledge of Bible history. Through them, we gain some sense of the circumstances the apostles encountered among the early Christians. They tell us, for example, about some of the false teachings, or *heresies,* that were leading certain believers astray from the truths taught by Christ.

The epistles also note the sources of conflicts among members of the local churches, which often grew out of disagreements over Christian teaching and practice. They provide hints about how the churches were structured, how the apostles ministered, and how the people worshipped. And they take us deeper into the minds, the hearts, and even the personalities of their authors.

A Vision of Hope and Comfort

The last book in the Bible, the Book of Revelation, was written by John. In it, he recorded for God's people a startling vision that he had received from heaven. The book has many perplexing details, so Christians have debated for two thousand years the exact meaning of certain parts of the book.

Even so, the main message of the vision is clear: No matter how many persecutions and other difficulties the Church may suffer, Jesus is the Lord of history. When the world at last comes to an end, He and His people will be triumphant over the Devil and his allies.

As we look forward to that bright destiny, the Book of Revelation tells us, God calls us to be faithful and fervent followers of His Son. That way we can come to enjoy His blessed fellowship in heaven forever, with all the angels and the saints. Such a vision of comfort and hope provides the perfect ending for the grand and glorious story of the Bible.

THE BOOKS OF THE NEW TESTAMENT

Matthew
Mark
Luke
John
Acts
Romans
1 Corinthians
2 Corinthians
Galatians
Ephesians
Philippians
Colossians
1 Thessalonians
2 Thessalonians
1 Timothy
2 Timothy
Titus
Philemon
Hebrews
James
1 Peter
2 Peter
1 John
2 John
3 John
Jude
Revelation

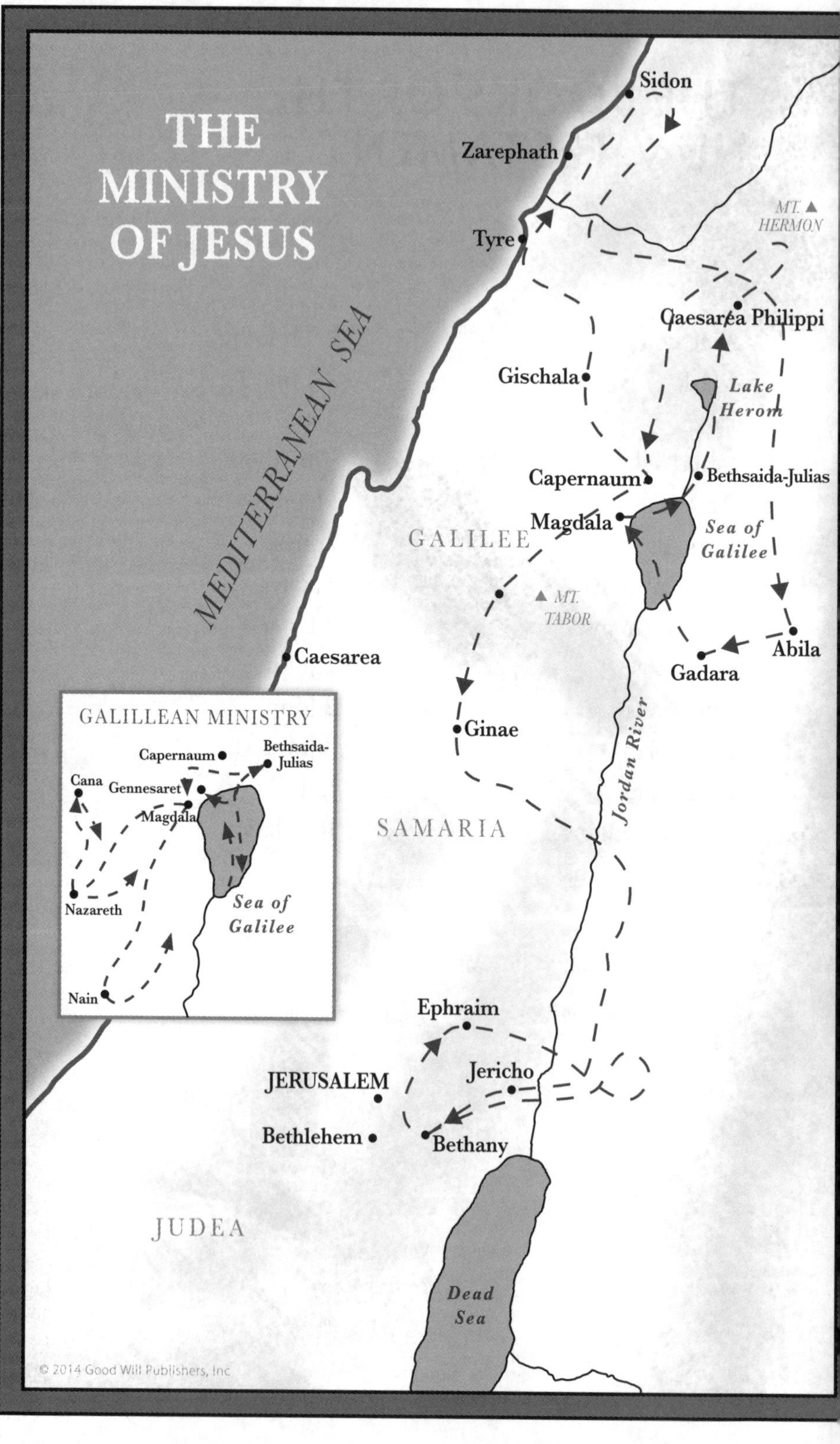
THE MINISTRY OF JESUS
MEDITERRANEAN SEA
Sidon
Zarephath
Tyre
MT. HERMON
Caesarea Philippi
Gischala
Lake Herom
Capernaum
Bethsaida-Julias
Magdala
GALILEE
Sea of Galilee
MT. TABOR
Abila
Gadara
Caesarea
Ginae
Jordan River
SAMARIA
GALILLEAN MINISTRY
Capernaum
Bethsaida-Julias
Cana
Gennesaret
Magdala
Nazareth
Sea of Galilee
Nain
Ephraim
Jericho
JERUSALEM
Bethlehem
Bethany
JUDEA
Dead Sea

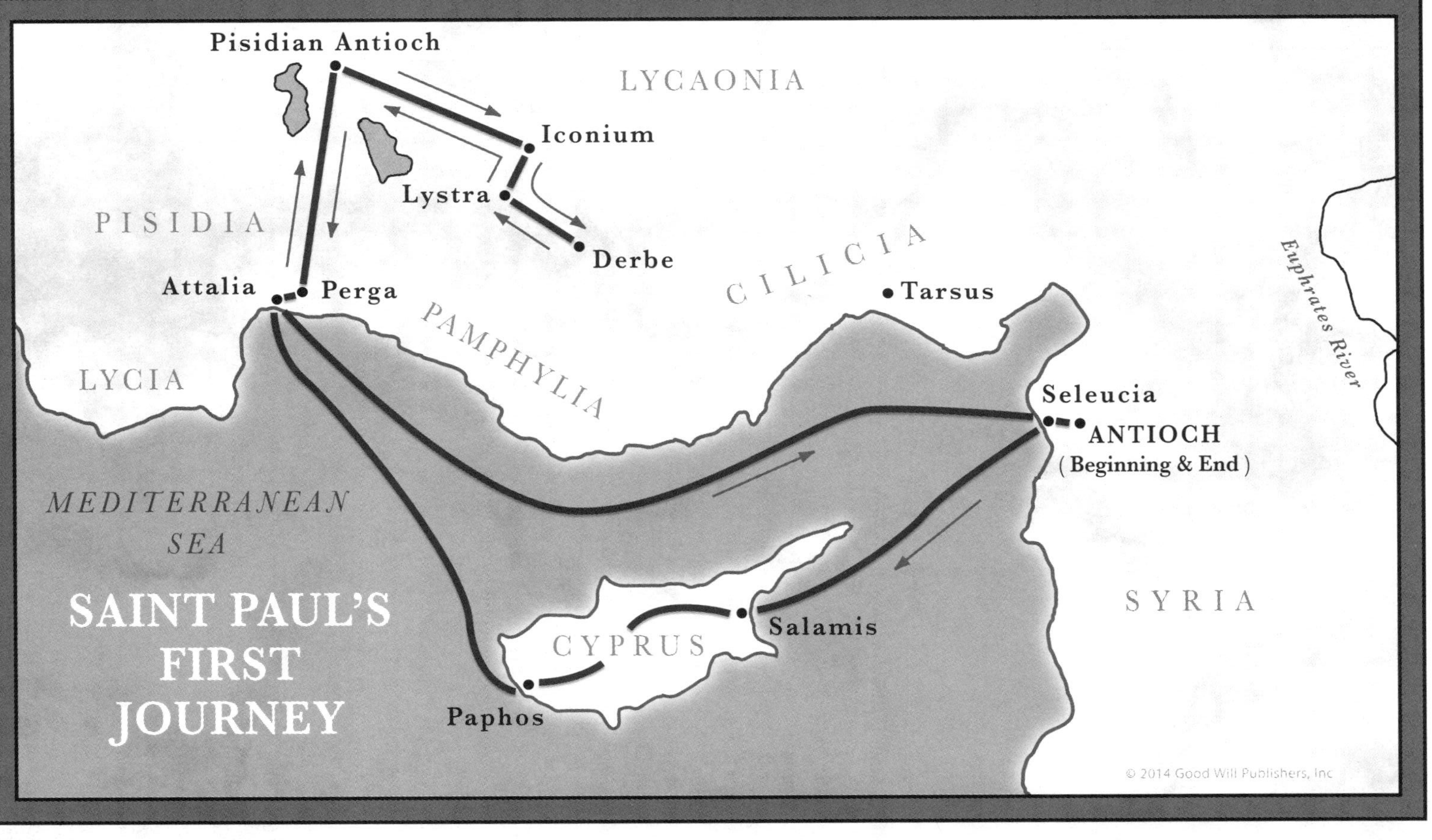
SAINT PAUL'S
FIRST
JOURNEY
Pisidian Antioch
LYCAONIA
Iconium
Lystra
Derbe
PISIDIA
Attalia
Perga
LYCIA
PAMPHYLIA
CILICIA
Tarsus
Euphrates River
Seleucia
ANTIOCH
(Beginning & End)
MEDITERRANEAN
SEA
CYPRUS
Salamis
Paphos
SYRIA
© 2014 Good Will Publishers, Inc

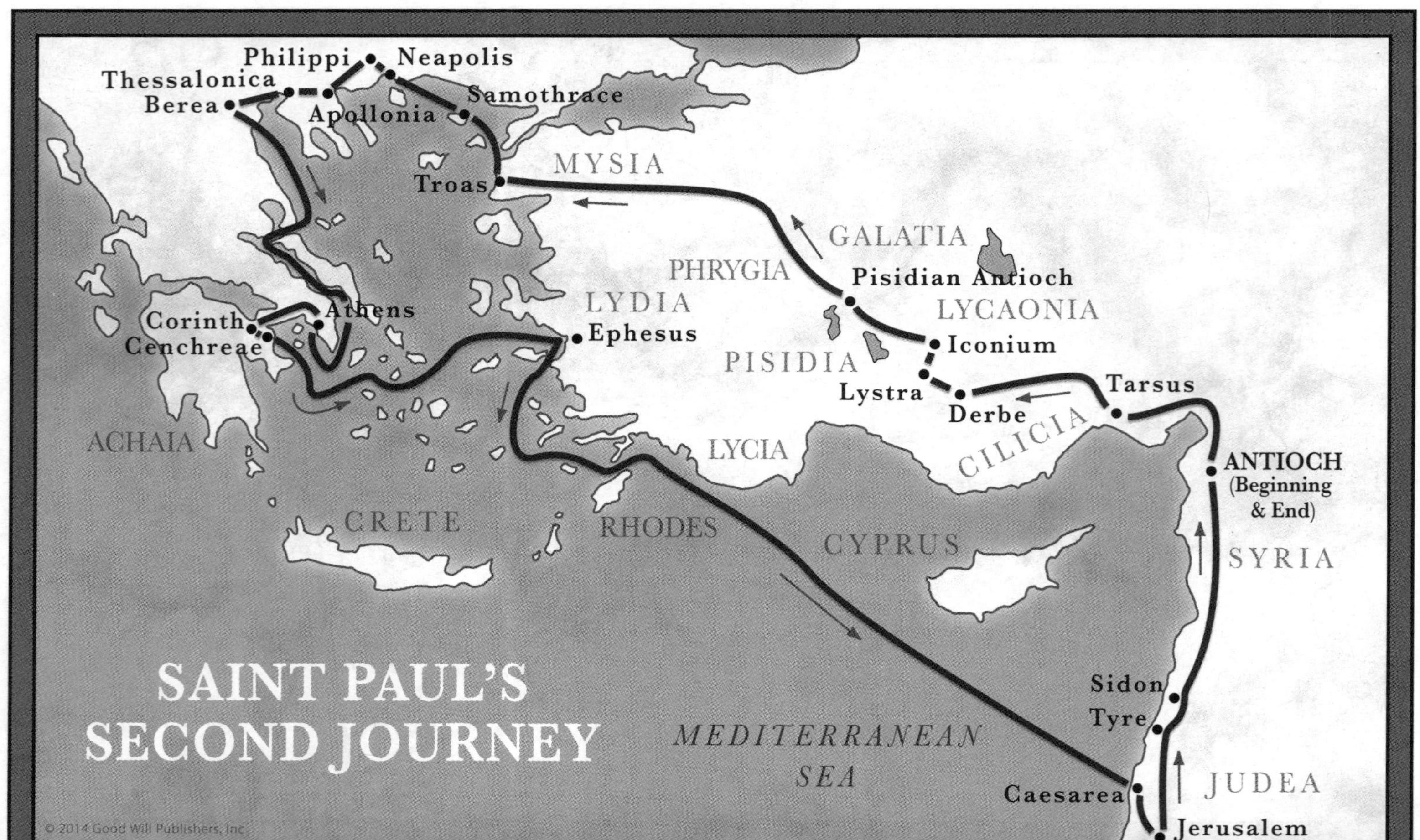
SAINT PAUL'S
SECOND JOURNEY
Philippi
Neapolis
Thessalonica
Samothrace
Berea
Apollonia
MYSIA
Troas
GALATIA
PHRYGIA
Pisidian Antioch
LYDIA
LYCAONIA
Corinth
Athens
Cenchreae
Ephesus
Iconium
PISIDIA
Lystra
Tarsus
Derbe
ACHAIA
LYCIA
CILICIA
ANTIOCH
(Beginning
& End)
CRETE
RHODES
CYPRUS
SYRIA
Sidon
Tyre
MEDITERRANEAN
SEA
JUDEA
Caesarea
Jerusalem

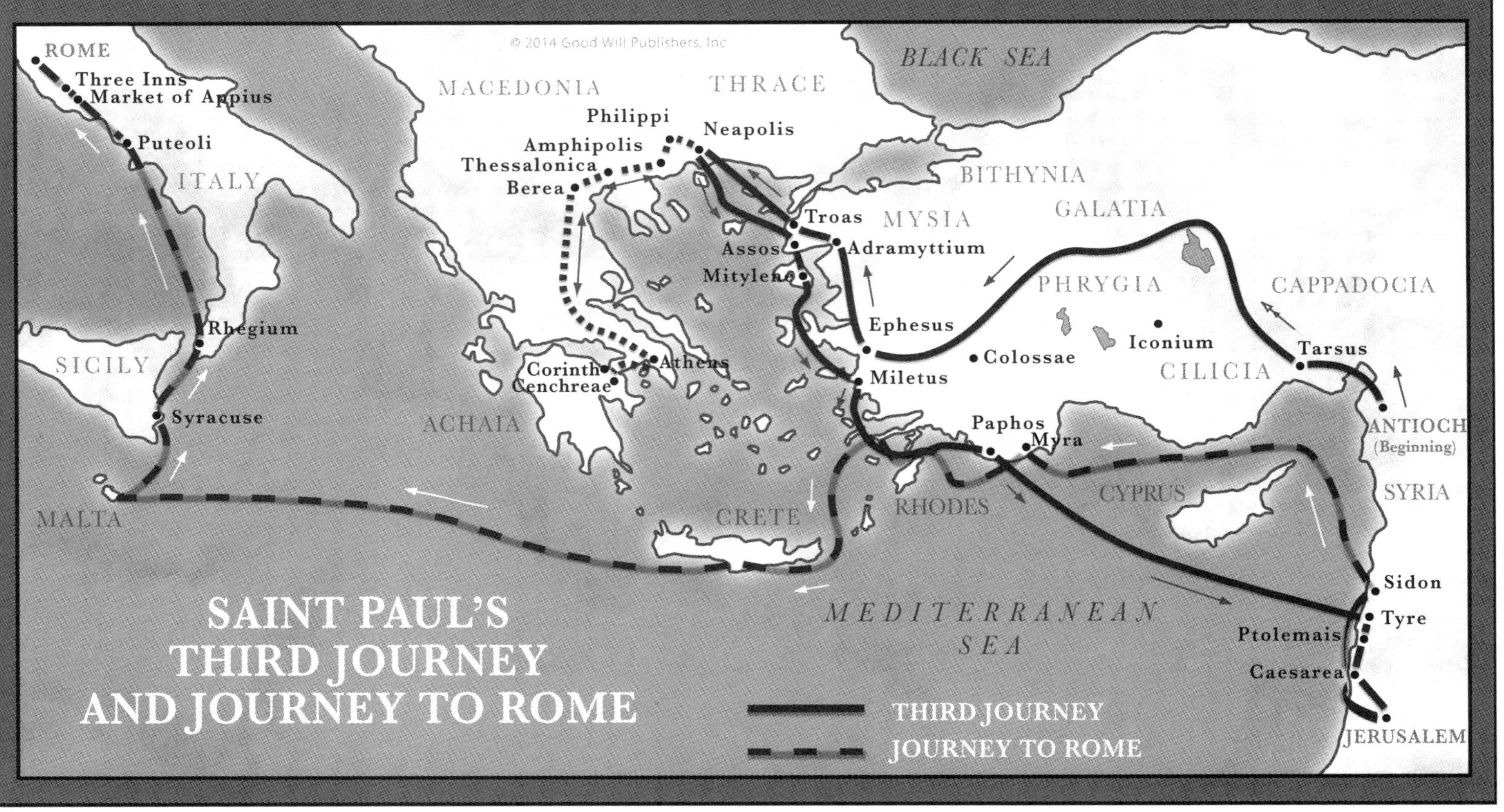

SAINT PAUL'S
THIRD JOURNEY
AND JOURNEY TO ROME
THIRD JOURNEY
JOURNEY TO ROME
© 2014 Good Will Publishers, Inc
ROME
Three Inns
Market of Appius
Puteoli
ITALY
Rhegium
SICILY
Syracuse
MALTA
MACEDONIA
THRACE
BLACK SEA
Philippi
Neapolis
Amphipolis
Thessalonica
Berea
Corinth
Cenchreae
Athens
ACHAIA
CRETE
Troas
Assos
Mitylene
Adramyttium
MYSIA
BITHYNIA
GALATIA
PHRYGIA
Ephesus
Colossae
Iconium
Miletus
CAPPADOCIA
Tarsus
CILICIA
Paphos
Myra
RHODES
CYPRUS
ANTIOCH
(Beginning)
SYRIA
Sidon
Tyre
Ptolemais
Caesarea
JERUSALEM
MEDITERRANEAN
SEA

INDEX

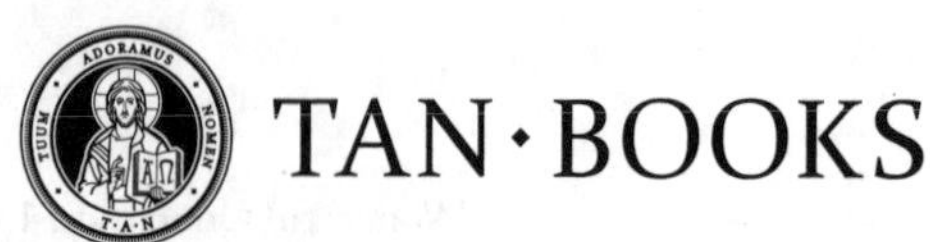

TAN Books was founded in 1967 to preserve the spiritual, intellectual and liturgical traditions of the Catholic Church. At a critical moment in history TAN kept alive the great classics of the Faith and drew many to the Church. In 2008 TAN was acquired by Saint Benedict Press. Today TAN continues its mission to a new generation of readers.

From its earliest days TAN has published a range of booklets that teach and defend the Faith. Through partnerships with organizations, apostolates, and mission-minded individuals, well over 10 million TAN booklets have been distributed.

More recently, TAN has expanded its publishing with the launch of Catholic calendars and daily planners—as well as Bibles, fiction, and multimedia products through its sister imprints Catholic Courses (CatholicCourses.com) and Saint Benedict Press (SaintBenedictPress.com). In 2015, TAN Homeschool became the latest addition to the TAN family, preserving the Faith for the next generation of Catholics (www.TANHomeschool.com).

Today TAN publishes over 500 titles in the areas of theology, prayer, devotions, doctrine, Church history, and the lives of the saints. TAN books are published in multiple languages and found throughout the world in schools, parishes, bookstores and homes.